# The Essential Guide to
# Being Hungarian
## 50 Facts & Facets of Nationhood

The Essential Guide to

# Being Hungarian

50 Facts & Facets of Nationhood

### Edited by
István Bori

*with*
Noémi Kiss
Péter Rácz
Gábor Vaderna

### Articles by

| | |
|---|---|
| Csilla Bakody | Orsolya Nádor |
| István Bori | Szabolcs Parragh |
| Nóra Csontos | Péter Rácz |
| Noémi Kiss | Katalin Suzuki Berkes |
| Jolán Mann | Adrienn Szentesi |
| Ádám Masát | Gábor Vaderna |

*Translated from the Hungarian by*
*Paul Olchváry*

NEW EUROPE
BOOKS

Published by New Europe Books, 2012
North Adams, Massachusetts 01247
www.NewEuropeBooks.com

Copyright © 2012 the authors
Copyright © 2012 the editors
Cover design © 2012 Oszkár Boskovitz

English translation © 2012 Paul Olchváry

Originally published in Hungary—in Hungarian in 2005 (Milyen a magyar . . . ?)
and in English in 2006—by L'Harmattan Press, Budapest, in cooperation with the
Bálint Balassi Hungarian Cultural Institute.

ISBN 978-0-9825781-0-0

Images on these pages © Shutterstock:
6, 26, 38, 39, 58, 101, 106, 108, 116, 146, 149, 156, 168, 178, 181

The typeface of the main text in this book is truly Hungarian: Pannon Antikva
(Edit Zigány, 1972 & Oszkár Boskovitz, 2001)

Library of Congress Cataloging-in-Publication Data

Milyen a magyar—? English

The essential guide to being Hungarian : 50 facts & facets of nationhood edited by
István Bori; with Noémi Kiss, Péter Rácz, Gábor Vaderna ; articles by Csilla Bakody ...
[et al.]; translated from the Hungarian by Paul Olchváry.

p. cm.

"Originally published in Hungary in Hungarian in 2005: Milyen a Magyar—?"
ISBN 978-0-9825781-0-0 (alk. paper)

1. National characteristics, Hungarian. 2. Hungary—Civilization. I. Bori, István II. Bori,
István. III. Kiss, Noémi, 1974- IV. Rácz, I. Péter, 1974- V. Bakody, Csilla. VI. Olchváry,
Paul. VII. Title.

DB919.15.M5513 2012

943.9--dc23

2012007548

Printed in the United States of America.

10 9 8 7 6 5 4 3 2 1

# Contents

## Publisher's Note

*If there are three Hungarians in a room, so goes a saying, they will belong to four political parties. Mercifully, this guide, which ostensibly has little to do with politics, seeks to be more a work of practical reference than one of commentary. That said, it does represent the individual efforts of twelve Hungarians to take on the daunting task of encapsulating, each in roughly four pages or less—and in no-holds-barred, candid terms where a subject is particularly subject to subjectivity— certain essentials of that elusive entity, the Hungarian mind; this, with the understanding that the publisher will generally refrain from injecting his own favorite facts & facets. In those cases where widely recognized facts are readily available, the authors provide these, in necessarily condensed form. But where a subject is one that lends itself to rumination over a shot or two of pálinka, best reach for the bottle! The kind reader is asked to take a gulp (or drop us a line) when an author fails to mention the one, two, or more other people, places, or whatever that seems a sin against the Hungarian nation to have omitted, otherwise departs from the reader's take on a specific sphere of life, or strays from the "politically correct." With that, we say, Egészségükre!—Cheers!*

Detail of Árpád Feszty's (1856–1914) cyclorama commemorating the 1000th anniversary of the Magyar conquest of the Carpathian Basin (see chapter 20, "Paintings")

# editors' preface

"They pass the time mainly by looking forward into the past," says Jimmy Porter about his father-in-law and his father-in-law's generation in John Osborne's play *Look Back in Anger.* This observation characterizes not only an age group but also a people—namely, the Hungarians. The submissions to an essay competition Budapest's Bálint Balassi Hungarian Cultural Institute (since renamed the Balassi Institute) held for non-Hungarians soon after the thousandth anniversary of Hungary's statehood (or, back in the year 1000, Pope-sanctioned kingdomhood) bore this out. Faced with the question "What are Hungarians like?", the respondents—who necessarily observe us Magyars from a distance, but in some cases dwell among us—observed, among other things, that Hungarians devote a staggering amount of attention to the past; indeed, they pour out onto the streets, flagrantly and loudly, several times a year in an effort to conjure up notable historical events.

What has this nation reaped from the past thousand years, and just what do Hungarians wish to reveal of themselves to those who do not share their cultural heritage? This book mines stereotypes for all they're worth, while also reflecting on whether non-Hungarians think the same things about us as we think about ourselves.

*The Essential Guide to Being Hungarian* comprises fifty short articles by a range of scholars—literary historians, linguists, historians, geographers, folklorists, and so on—who've been teaching non-Hungarian students for years in the Institute's Hungarian studies program. The intriguing questions that have emerged in conversations with these students led our authors to begin examining the meaning of "Hungarianness" in the broad sense of the word. What is to be Hungarian? They sought to answer this question through a good hard look at all the cultural and material heritage that is characteristically "Hungarian," at least in the general estimation of the world at large. The aim was neither to "scientifically" construct · a portrait of Hungarianness—a hopeless endeavor, in any case—nor to impose on others our notions of what it is to be Hungarian. To the contrary. Taking stereotypes as its starting point, this guide aims to jibe with today's "globalized" world—which seeks a continual exchange of traits among peoples rather than a hierarchy of cultures.

Our book seeks, therefore, to shed light on such quintessential facts and facets of Hungarian nationhood that, while self-evident within the fold of Hungarian culture, are presumably unfamiliar to non-Hungarians or are interpreted differently by them. We hope the fifty topics presented succinctly herein—topics we selected from a much longer list—conveys a broad cross-section of what it is to be Hungarian in the present day. Readers will gain insight into various areas of Hungarian culture and society, into the living and nonliving treasures of a nation's natural surroundings, into the shaping of contemporary Hungarian public life and public thinking; and, moreover, into the mysteries of the "Hungarian soul." Making appearances in these thematically arranged articles are those historical figures—from artists to thinkers, statesmen to sportsmen—whose lives and achievements Hungarians consider essential aspects of their nation's psyche, who serve as national role models; and who, in some cases, saw world fame. The book also presents emblematic figures of the present-day.

This book is for anyone who has ever wondered, "Hungarian? What's that?" More seriously, The Essential Guide to Being Hungarian is for anyone interested in or intrigued by Hungarian culture—whether travelers or non-Hungarian citizens who reside in Hungary, whether of Hungarian extraction or not, wherever they may be in the world. In short, it is for all readers who wish to quickly get a handle on the elusive essence of being Hungarian.

*I am Magyar. A somber soul, that's me:*
*Like our fiddles' first strains of play.*
*A smile flits across my lips occasionally,*
*But rarely can you hear me laugh away.*
*When bliss comes over me, when its glow*
*Visits my eyes, tears surge like a sea.*
*But my face seems cheerful in times of woe,*
*Because I don't want you to pity me.**

# soul

## Gábor Vaderna

The words above comprise the answer that Hungary's most famous nineteenth-century poet gave to the question, "What is the Hungarian soul?" Sándor Petőfi was a romantic to the bone—and so he is talking about himself, he is doggedly proud, and he adores extremes. But how can one simultaneously laugh and cry? This, Petőfi does not reveal. The Hungarian soul is secretive, after all.

The Hungarian is proud of his homeland (or *her* homeland, but for the sake of simplicity, and to reflect the way most Hungarians would imagine it, for better or for worse, let's keep saying "he"). When he meets a foreigner, he tells him all about his nation's catastrophe-laden history. He tells the story of the Magyars' grand conquest of the Carpathian Basin way back in 896; of the Turks occupying our land more than five-hundred years later for one-hundred fifty years; of calling the Austrians "in-laws," since we lived in one single monarchy of a country; of how historical Hungary fell to pieces in the twentieth century; of how communism came and went; and of how, these days, we've got democracy and, yes, of how we're in the belly of that benign beast we call the European Union. He knows it all, and he accepts responsibility for it all.

The Hungarian knows his past. The Hungarian is proud of his culture. Even if he is often off-key, he can rattle off a few folksongs, like that. And you can bet your bottom dollar that he can recite more than a few classical Hungarian poems by heart, even if he sometimes blurts out only a line here or a stanza there. If we drop in on a Hungarian at home, we'll probably find his place chock full of books, most of which he's read, and some of which he will surely

*Translated by Paul Olchváry

read long before retirement. Contemporary literature might not be his cup of tea, but his bookshelf is brimming with the classics. And not only does he love to read, but sometimes he also dons his Sunday best and heads to the theater or the concert hall.

The Hungarian loves to eat . . . and eat . . . and eat. He loves cooking, too. On Sundays the family sits down for a feast. Beef soup, chicken paprikash with a heap of tiny egg-flour dumplings, and traditional pastry of some sort. Yes, on Sundays there's pastry, too. The Hungarian takes two servings of each course and he showers praise upon the chef. "I can't resist. I've just got to try some more of this luscious little chicken." In the afternoon he puts a palm to his belly. "I shouldn't have had so much." When it comes to eating, the Hungarian knows no bounds. When it comes to everything else, too. For example, the Hungarian loves to party it up. If he sets himself to drinking a couple of glasses' worth (of booze), why then, he's sure to do it like a real pro. He loves *pálinka*, that clear, potent spirit distilled from plums, pears, or some such fruit (except in the case of lower-cost, synthetically produced variations). He loves good wine. Beer, too, is close to his heart. And what's a mug of beer without a shot of his beloved herbal bitter, Unicum? What the Hungarian loves most of all, however, is if he can both eat *and* drink. What is more, he just loves it if he can also dance into the bargain. The Hungarian loves great big weddings, especially great big never-ending rural weddings, where the guests come and stay a while, too. There, the Hungarian finds everything he loves.

The Hungarian is lazy. If he is working on a deadline, it's a safe bet we can't expect any results until the last second. He loves his work, but he's not about to rush it, either. He is a master at always working at just the right pace. If he must, he speeds up; if need be, he slows down. The Hungarian loves to play hard to get, but he still won't believe it if he does something wrong. The Hungarian is, if be he must, surprisingly thorough.

The Hungarian is clever. He loves to think. He'd simplify all things logically if only he could, which means he's unwilling to bend even a blade of grass if doing so isn't really necessary. He loves games of logic. He thinks fast. He loves crosswords. He loves to play chess in the park, and he loves to watch folks play chess in the park. He is crazy about card games.

The Hungarian has problems up to his ears. He loves to complain. He is convinced that he, being Hungarian, gets the most disrespect in the whole wide world; that no one meets with more offence and suffers more than he, the Hungarian. But no one should imagine even for a moment that it's possible to gain any insight into a Hungarian's problems. No, the Hungarian is a true melancholic: he thinks a lot about himself but talks about this with few people indeed. The Hungarian is capable

Márk Rózsavölgyi (1789–1848), composer and violinist, "father of the csárdás"

of cursing in multitudinous ways, and rich ways at that, but it takes some doing to win his confidence enough so that he might spew his rage in front of our eyes.

A Hungarian's emotions run deep. When he talks seriously he thinks seriously, too. He just can't let loose at such times. Then again, he does sometimes think seriously about several things at the same time. What does he do at such times? Why, he laughs and he cries.

# fate

## Péter Rácz

*Fate*—a weighty, somber word. *Sors* in Hungarian. Whereas even in Hungary's national anthem—the *Himnusz*—the word *balsors* (literally: ill fate) in fact means "misfortune." If we precede it with one of its more frequently used modifiers, *magyar*, yielding *magyar sors* (Hungarian fate), hardly is there a soul in this nation of ours who imagines happiness or good fortune. Hungarian.

Generally speaking, to be Hungarian is to be dealt a real blow by life—as quite a few of our compatriots do in fact believe. It is misfortune itself; it is to be an outcast, persecuted, beaten, forced into migration (whether abroad or to elsewhere in Hungary), exist as a minority, live in penury or backwardness; it is to be orphaned, to be misunderstood in life. This "Gloomy Hungarian Fate" is nothing new—it is indeed the title of a 1908 painting by János Tornyai (1869–1936)—and to this day it endures, albeit primarily in the vocabulary of those particularly, piercingly, publicly patriotic folks who make a big to-do about being Hungarian.

At the same time, the very use of the term resonates with a bit of Hungarian pride, too. That is: we defended (Christian) Europe from the Turks, we suffered "the most," we rebelled the most often against our oppressors, and we endured at the crossroads of East and West. Never mind that one look at a map of Europe is enough to show that history was no kinder to other peoples, either.

We are given to highlighting those passages of our history during which we were under foreign occupation: the destruction wrought by the Mongols during the Tatar invasion of 1241, Turkish domination in the sixteenth and seventeenth centuries; and, later, Habsburg rule. One trauma that abides palpably to this day, however, is the Treaty of Trianon that followed World War I and the collapse of the Austro-Hungarian Monarchy, in 1920 to be precise. Under its terms, Hungary was forced to cede two-thirds of its territory to neighboring countries. Indeed, this traumatic loss lives on vividly in the memories of Hungarians today. Many families have relatives or acquaintances from among the ethnic Hungarians who live on the far side of the border, and at the same time various other everyday circumstances of life in Hungary likewise preserve the memory of a richer past when the nation was "whole." Just a few of the many linguistic memories include *kolozsvári káposzta* (i.e., Kolozsvár cabbage, Kolozsvár being the Hungarian name for the city of Cluj-Napoca, in present-day Romania) and *pozsonyi kifli* (Pozsony crescent, a walnut and poppy-seed filled pastry named after the Hungarian name for the now-Slovak capital of Bratislava). And then there is administrative and or economic lingo, such as "natural assets lost with annexed territories," which suggests something unmistakably geographic-historic pertaining to Hungary.

That's not even to mention that so much of our nation's transportation infrastructure invariably reminds Hungarians of what has been lost: road and rail networks with Budapest at their center fan outward toward cities that in Hungary are naturally known by their Hungarian names: Kassa (Košice, Slovakia), Nagyvárad (Oradea, Romania), Kolozsvár (Cluj-Napoca, Romania), and Szabadka (Subotica, Serbia). The resultant sense of historical injustice that abides in modern-day Hungarian minds not only reinforces what had been a predisposition to look to the past even before Trianon. It is also an obstacle to nurturing friendly relations with our neighbors.

Meanwhile, yet other defining and sometimes even successful eras of Hungarian history (whether that of Hungary's first king, Stephen, or the Renaissance-minded Matthias Corvinus) give—should give—Hungarians less reason to complain.

Hungarians have an abiding sense of their own singularity stemming from their Asian origins, their unusual arrival in the

Carpathian Basin (*honfoglalás*, which literally means "Settlement of the Homeland" but is generally called "Conquest" in English), failed historical endeavors (lost revolutions, struggles for freedom, world wars); and, last but not least, a language that confounds most everyone except Hungarians. At the same time, they are not exactly adept at critical thinking, at the self-reflection that might well allow for better accommodation to the prevailing circumstances of the present day. For example, consider how many Hungarians tend to think—or, more to the point, not to think—about the policies that led to their nation's inglorious participation in World War II; how the decades-long Kádár era that followed the 1956 Revolution could not have endured for so long without conscious public complicity; and of course there is the propensity of no few Magyars for boundless self-praise and self-pity alike.

The correlation in the Hungarian mind between fate and misfortune can be traced to the age of Romanticism: The eighteenth-century poet Dániel Berzsenyi derided what he saw as his compatriots' fatefully indolent, decadent frame of mind. In the mid-nineteenth century, Ferenc Kölcsey made fate as misfortune a stirring motif of the national anthem, the *Himnusz*; as did Mihály Vörösmarty in his seminal poem "Szózat" (*Summons*), which functions as an alternative national anthem. And that century's most famously Romantic Hungarian poet of all, Sándor Petőfi, in his poem "Sors, nyiss nekem tért" (Fate, Give Me Space), asked fate to give him the opportunity to "do something for mankind." In the early-twentieth century, Endre Ady began his poem "Szép, magyar sors" (Lovely, Hungarian Fate): "There's some great-great Fate, Reason, Purpose indeed    Some great-great ancient lesson    For small nations to heed." Other great Hungarian poets and writers of the twentieth century, from Mihály Babits to István Örkény, likewise strove to articulate the nature of the Hungarian fate, and indeed their literary voices are generally tragic, sometimes grotesque. It was the political theorist István Bibó (1911–1979) who finally adopted a sober, objective tone in analyzing the Hungarian fate in its regional, Eastern-Central European context.

At the same time, fate appears in more balanced form in the sayings and adages of this melancholic people who are not exactly famous for being rational—from *sorsára hagy* (leave to one's fate) to *gyors, mint a sors* (fast, like fate) to *A sorsát senki sem kerülheti el* (No one can evade their fate).

# landscape

## István Bori

On witnessing Hungary's national team led by Ferenc Puskás stage one helluva soccer struggle against the Germans in Basel, Switzerland, on June 20, 1954, the German television commentator talked with resignation of an "onslaught from the steppes." (See the final chapter of this guide, "Athlete;" for everything you ever wanted to know about Puskás.) This succinct characterization of Hungarianness embraces all those notions of the Hungarian landscape and of history that existed then, and exist today, in the minds of no few German tourists in Hungary: the Magyar armies that, freshly arrived from the steppes, proceeded in the tenth century to terrorize Western Europe (making their way as far as St. Gallen, in present-day Switzerland, where they ravaged a Benedictine monastery in 962); and, of course, the enduring image of barren, flat open country bereft of high mountains.

How deceptive, this image! Few Hungarians today have ever been on horseback, and fewer still have ever shot arrows backward as did their predecessors when seeking to ensnare their enemies. Even Hungary's famous *puszta*—that flat, grassy landscape that seems to stretch endlessly toward the horizon—truly exists in but one particular place, in the Hortobágy of the country's western, Alföld region. The present-day image (and reality) of the Hortobágy as a somewhat grassy but mostly parched flatland is, however, not a natural condition, but the consequence of human activity, of agriculture. Indeed, this steppe was originally brimming with forests and open woodlands. But it transformed through centuries of ravaged forests, broken soil, irrigation systems built, and vast herds of cattle and flocks of sheep that grazed everything in sight. Nineteenth-century efforts to regulate the flow of the River Tisza—to straighten out all its many bends, to put a squeeze on the unbridled river by building locks—didn't help matters, either, in this respect. In short, it shut off the taps of that annually reproducing, watery wilderness that was, until then, yet another singularity of the Hortobágy. The immense wealth of bird life that once occurred here is today to be found only in and around fishing lakes of varying size that enjoy heightened protection and that break the puszta's overall monotony. Not that this particular monotony is dull. Far from it. It's enough to experience a sunrise and, say, a passing summer storm replete with gusts of wind, or to glimpse a mirage unfolding in the summer heat.

While all this might be interesting even to those accustomed to mountain peaks and deep winding valleys, such people will hardly find it thrilling. They would be well advised to venture into

Hungarian gray cattle on the Hortobágy (see chapter 5, "Livestock")

western Hungary (i.e., west of the Danube), where they can delight in hills that, while certainly not Alps, do comprise humble ranges of varying elevations. That's not to mention that Central Europe's largest lake, the Balaton, is to be found in this region. A wide swath of northern Hungary is also covered by wild, forested hills, by the way.

But back to the pustza as emblematic of what others, and

Hungarians, too, often think of as *Hungarian*. The great nineteenth-century poet Sándor Petőfi did much to underpin the romance of his country's eastern plains. Take for example his work, "A csárda romjai" (Ruins of the Country Tavern): "That hill country with its slopes and vales so rough / Is a book whose countless pages turn and turn you must, / But you, my Alföld, where beyond the hills no more hills arise, / Are like a missive opened wide."

Indeed, the flat open country of the puszta simultaneously evokes a sense not only of freedom and vulnerability, but also of constancy. This stirs the memory of those times past when Hungarians' ancestors lived a nomadic life on the endless grassy flatlands of Eurasia. These times are now associated in the Hungarian mind with an image of freedom free of all external influences.

Of course, ancient times often seem lovelier than they were in reality. The nomadic life of livestock breeding was not merely a matter of aimless rambling. To the contrary, its limits were palpable indeed. This was an existence subject to the whims of the weather, to finding well-protected watering holes and shelters, and to the location of other nomadic peoples. It had a know able order to it, one whose rules guaranteed life and survival. It's not by chance that leadership among peoples of the puszta was inherited based on seniority. The torch could be passed on only to the oldest and most experienced member of the family. History was to confirm the success of this system more than once. We need think only of those Magyars whose tenth-century pillaging excursions inspired terror in Western Europe; and of the fact that to this day, it is this image of the Magyars—as a wild, equestrian-nomadic people—that endures in the public mind.

# horse

## Noémi Kiss

Hungarians have, over the centuries, been among Europe's most celebrated equestrians. But do we live up to this reputation even today? Sure, we conquered the Carpathian Basin on the backs of Asian horses, and we're still proud of our equines even though only a fraction of our onetime wealth of breeds still exists. In Hungary these days, the horse is used mainly for sport, while further to the east it is still a beast of burden. Alas, decades of state socialism did no good at all to the cause of Hungarian horse-breeding, though in recent years this sub-sector of the economy has begun to blossom anew, as it does seem to be a good investment. And perhaps it is not by chance that, for years, Hungarian athletes led the world in their finesse on the pommel horse.

What would Hungarian history be without the horse? From King Stephen back around the year 1000 to Regent Miklós Horthy more than 900 years later (the "Admiral without a Ship" *did* have a horse), these two most celebrated horse lovers from our history books devoted special attention to the establishment, maintenance, and development of Hungarian horse-breeding. Queen Maria Theresa of the Habsburg clan (1740–1780) was just crazy about horses, nay, legends have it that she rode them right into her bed. The legendarily beautiful Queen Elizabeth ("Sisi"), wife of Austrian Emperor Francis Joseph I (1848–1916; King of Hungary from 1867) and regarded by Hungarians as their nation's "Guardian Angel" owing to her love of Hungary, visited the small town of Gödöllő east of Budapest for years primarily for its horses. Sultry rumors had it that Count Gyula Andrássy, a statesman and a Hungarian prime minister, was given to accompanying her on her rides.

Hungary's most celebrated horse of all, the indomitable, invincible wonder mare Kincsem (My Treasure), entered this world in 1877 on the country estate of Count Ernő Blaskovich in the sleepy town of Tápiószentmárton. Her career comprised fifty-four races, all of which she won. To this day she is one of the world's most famous racehorses. A life-size bronze statue of her was erected in 1977 by the main entrance of the aptly named Kincsem Park, Budapest's main race track.

Breeding-wise, horses always were Hungary's most important animals of all, if of course you exclude cattle from consideration.

This particular sector really took off in Hungary beginning in the mid-nineteenth century. Our horses reaped laurels at major international competitions, and that is when the *Magyar Állami Ménes* (Hungarian State Stud Farm) was established as a home for native Hungarian breeds.

Our nation's horses are typically stout, brawny, hardened, fleet, and

The indomitable, invincible nineteenth-century wonder mare Kincsem (My Treasure)

sturdy to boot. True, they're none too high and none too graceful, and what with their shapes, more squat than anything, they would hardly stand a chance of winning a beauty contest. The ancient breed we brought with us from Asia was a stocky but exceptionally sturdy, heavy-duty creature. And, as history would have it, it crossbred with Polish, Turkish, and Serbian breeds. The breed the State Stud Farm later excelled at was developed from English, Arabian, and Lipizzaner horses.

A whole institution of breeding estates and farms developed in the nineteenth century as Hungary's population of quality horses grew and grew. By century's end, some such farms were worth a fortune. Although by then the growth rate had waned a bit in numerical terms, a more focused effort gathered force to nurture and propagate certain breeds. At first, horses were valued chiefly for their labor, whether as steeds or to carry or pull heavy loads. Back in the days of the Conquest in 896 the horse, to the Magyars, was also a sacrificial animal. In the Middle Ages, its flesh was eaten, too. However, the Roman Catholic Church later banned the consumption of horse meat. These days horse meat even features on the menus of a few restaurants in Hungary, though Hungarian horses have little to fear: few Hungarian humans savor the prospect of dining on horse.

During the twentieth century the Hungarian horse gradually lost its military value and its importance in transporting freight, and so today it is much more often raised for recreational riding or for racing. Hungary's present-day horse population is but a fraction of the two million the country was home to at the turn of the twentieth century. Horses are bred both at state-run stud farms and by private individuals. Four Hungarian stud farms in particular feature in the horse-breeding history books: the one in the town of Kisbér (western Hungary), which specialized in English horses; that in Bábolna (just north of Kisbér), where Arabians became the horses of choice; the largest such farm, in Mezőhegyes (eastern Hungary), which concentrated on the small, Nonius and Gidan breeds; and the stud farm in Fogaras (today in central Romania). Horse breeding requires substantial capital investment, but horses can bring sizable profits if the breeding is professional and the horses capable of competing internationally. As such, Hungarian thoroughbreds, like so many of their Hungarian human counterparts, have long made their way into the wider world, the biggest market traditionally having been North America.

# livestock

## Noémi Kiss

The animals we're talking about here are those either bred or otherwise introduced in Hungary to the point where they became indigenous. "*Livestock*" in English, *haszonállat* ("beneficial animal") in Hungarian—whatever the language, the name suggests that in exchange for providing such creatures with food and water, such beasts provide certain beneficial services to their human stewards. So then, Hungary's three best-known types of livestock are . . . (drum roll please) . . . the *mangalica* pig, the grey cattle, and the *racka* sheep. Each is by nature and disposition a semiwild, incorrigibly free-range beast. The flesh, the hide, and the hair of each is of exceptional quality.

The mangalica is one special pig. It was one of the head hogs even back in the good old days of Hungarian livestock breeding. Known all over Central and Eastern Europe, it is enjoying renewed popularity today on account of its lusciously marbled fat and, not least, savvy marketing that has persuaded consumers that it is downright healthy (not that it is actually "cholesterol free," as per one often heard claim). Also called the "bristly-haired hog"— and, by rural folk, the *szőrdisznó* (bristle-hog)—it was a one-of-a-kind source of fat and bacon in this region as far back as the nineteenth century. In accord with the new circumstances of the era, Hungary's mangalica developed from a local breed known as the *sumadia*. Its most celebrated center was a breeding farm owned by Joseph Anton Johann of Austria, Palatine of Hungary, in Kisinje, a small community in what was then Hungary and is today Romania. The mangalica's official "creation" story goes as follows: the archduke received a stock of ten sows and two boars in 1833 from Prince Miloš of Serbia. By 1850, in corn-rich areas of Hungary, the mangalica had supplanted an earlier, semi-wild, thinner-fleshed pig, and before long it was way ahead in numbers. This development was helped along by the creation of substantial new areas of grazing land in the region due to the draining of marshes and the cutting of forests.

Swineherds, shepherds, cowboys, and horseherds saw to managing these ancient breeds that were used to roaming freely and far afield. Initially the fattened animals were herded on foot to markets in Vienna and Prague. By the early 1900s, with the establishment of large-scale breeding facilities and with newer hybrids, the time involved in fattening a mangalica had waned substantially. The bristly-haired hogs were crossbred with international breeds including black (Cornwall) and mottled (Berkshire, Poland China) varieties. Officially speaking, the mangalica today comes in three shades: gray, red, and "swallow-bellied." Earlier records indicate that there used to be completely black and also brownish-gray varieties. Traditionally, however, the blond mangalica is the real McCoy. Its hair is thick and long, and curled in the winter like wood shavings, which is why rural folk also refer to it as the "woolly hog." In days past, the average mangalica weighed in at 200 kilograms (440 pounds), of which 60–70 percent was fat when slaughtered. Its modern-day counterpart rings in at 150 kilos (330 pounds). Newborn piglets have striped backs.

On now from the mangalica to the Hungarian gray cattle, a docile beast that fell into favor chiefly for its meat. From the thirteenth century on, it was known in much of Central Europe as having the finest flesh of any cattle. In a modern-day sense it may be relatively safe to eat, as it has never received industrial feed nor has it ever been infected with BSE (i.e., "mad cow disease").

Several theories speak to the origins of the gray cattle. According to one, the species inhabited the Carpathian Basin even before the Magyar Conquest. Yet another strain of thought is that it was precisely the Magyars who brought it with them from Asia. What is certain is that the Hungarian gray cattle belongs genetically to the Podolian group of the European wild cattle, *Bos primigenius*, of which it is the most famous, mid-weight representative. It rings in at around 500 kilograms (1,100 pounds) and attains a height of 135 centimeters (53 inches). Hungary's stock of such free-roaming cattle survived both the Tatar invasion and the Turkish occupation, and for centuries played a vital role in the nation's economy. As was the case with mangalica pigs, oxen raised on Hungary's parched, saline flatlands were driven by foot to Western markets, from Vienna to Nuremberg to Venice, both because of the lack of refrigeration and, not least, to keep them moving. The best years saw more than 100,000 head of cattle exported this way. The oxen were especially favored for their dry and delectable flesh, whose fibers contain relatively few fat deposits.

Last but not least, the racka sheep: In Hungary, the racka is also called the *igazi* (real) sheep or the Hortobágy sheep. This Hungarian peasants' sheep, which at the turn of the twentieth century was found primarily on eastern Hungary's Alföld great plain and further east in Transylvania, adapts exceptionally to whatever local climate it happens to find itself in. The racka comes in both white and black, the latter variety being hauntingly beautiful, what with its seemingly proud stature. Averaging 45 kilograms (99 pounds), it annually produces almost 2 kilograms (4.4 pounds) of wool but only 35–40 liters (37–42 quarts) of milk, which in turn yields 7–8 kilograms (15–18 pounds) of cheese. It fattens well and its meat is savory, but never was it really kept for meat. More important, its hide was used to make the long peasant cloaks and coats stereotypically associated with life on the Hungarian plains, and the hides of young sheep were used to make that distinctively high fur cap called the *bagolysüveg* (owl cap).

The racka sheep is easy to recognize from its graceful, antelope-like horns, which extend straight upward and outward and are twisted tightly around their axis. The lamb's fur is of a quality comparable to that of its Persian counterpart. The racka is subject to a breeding program unique to the world, with its numbers presently at a few thousand, just enough to sustain the breed. The city of Debrecen, at the edge of the Hortobágy in eastern Hungary, is home to the Racka Sheep Breeding Association. A small number of rackas occur in Romania, too, at the southern edge of Translyvania; and related breeds are also found in Romania, both further to the east in Transylvania and beyond. Related breeds have reportedly been found in China as well, though little is known of their origins. All that is certain is that the Magyars brought the racka sheep with them when they settled the Carpathian Basin. But, oddly enough, at that point the sheep were not yet endowed with their twisted horns—a phenomenon that probably unfolded in the fourteenth and fifteenth centuries.

After 1945, the breeding associations that had previously existed in Hungary ceased, and the increasing prevalence of the common meat hog almost completely decimated the country's native livestock. It wasn't until 1973 that the government finally granted protected status to the remaining such animals. Since then, it is safe to say that each of these breeds—the mangalica pig, the gray cattle, and the racka sheep—is better looked after than any other livestock in our nation. Indeed, visitors to Hungary can see living examples of all three at the Puszta Game Farm on the Hortobágy, which can be seen virtually at www.pusztaiallatpark.hu.

# disease

## Ádám Masát

Rarely in the history of medicine has an illness been named after a nation, but we Hungarians can say with bitter pride: here's another one of those things fate has doled out our share of. True, we're not alone. For example, rickets is also called the English Disease. Now, supposedly the only thing that rickets has to do with the English is that English doctors first managed to diagnose it. Why, then, was *morbus hungaricus* named for us, of all people? And what disease does this term refer to, after all?

Those older folks who recall the malady's "golden age" are quick to respond: tuberculosis. The incidence of TB was so high in Hungary at one time—especially during the Austro-Hungarian Monarchy and through the first half of the twentieth century—that all over the world tuberculosis was dubbed *morbus hungaricus*. According to some figures, this common disease, which was also called "consumption," took between 40,000 and 50,000 lives in Hungary annually under Emperor Franz Joseph, and only with the introduction of required inoculations for newborns was it finally brought into check. In this light, it is especially surprising that the term *morbus hungaricus* is in fact the product neither of the nineteenth nor the twentieth century—but that a physician from Marburg, Germany, had used this term in a thesis way back in the sixteenth century.

Here's why. On more than one occasion, epidemics broke out among the foreign troops that were often stationed on the territory of Hungary in the sixteenth and seventeenth centuries, when the country was divided into three parts. In particular, there emerged in the ranks of these armies-which were patched together with mercenaries from all corners of Europe, and which generally struggled against the Turks—a new epidemic previously unfamiliar to doctors. According to historical sources, the nameless contagion wreaked terrible devastation especially after Buda was recaptured from the Turks in 1686, and the mercenaries then took it home and spread it in many reaches of the continent. The doctors, who were at a loss when it came to curing this infectious disease, named it *morbus hungaricus* on account of the place it emerged. Only that this disease was not the tuberculosis that spread in the twentieth century, but epidemic typhus. Thus, *morbus hungaricus* meant two different things in two different eras.

Of course, typhus and tuberculosis were not the only diseases that have wreaked havoc in Hungary. Sadly, our country is known in the developed world also in connection with other maladies. Beginning in the second half of the twentieth century, the term—or, perhaps more appropriately, the concept—*morbus hungaricus* has also come to embrace the somber fact that Hungarians are among the world's statistical leaders in alcoholism, overeating, heart and circulatory diseases, and, yes, suicide. Only since the political sea change that transpired in 1989–90 has a bit of improvement been noticeable on this front. Such is the irony of fate, however, that tuberculosis seems to have been making new inroads since around the turn of the millennium. Yes, TB is again rearing its head among our nation's increasing numbers of homeless, who are particularly susceptible to infection, and among other people whose health has been weakened due to malnourishment, alcoholism, or other ailments. In these respects, then, although we inhabit a modern society with decent health care, we Hungarians continue to be a disease-disposed lot. The question remains: is recovery on the horizon?

# world heritage

István Bori

UNESCO's list of World Heritage sites presently includes eight Hungarian natural and cultural landmarks. Let us take a virtual, concise, twenty-four hour tour to these places.

*00:00*
Travel to northern Hungary, to Aggtelek National Park. This is home to the entrance of Baradla-Domica, the most imposing cave in the karst hills along this stretch of Hungary's border with Slovakia. Humans have dwelled in the vicinity for thousands of years. Being midnight, outside it's still dark, but that's no problem, as we're visiting the realm of darkness, anyway—one of Europe's largest stalactite caves.

In 1825 this was still the world's longest mapped cave, although by the present day it has fallen a bit in this ranking. On descending, we see the monumental formations of the underground world, the colossal stalactites, the largest of which is the eighteen-meter high "Observatory." Here in the deep a person is alone, and cold, but enveloped by a boundless sense of calm. The only sound is that of dripping water—a little drop of Hungary.

*03:00*
We go on to southern Hungary, to the city of Pécs. Time travel to the foot of the Mecsek Hills, back to the Roman era. What's there to see in the cryptic silence of early morning? Ancient Christian crypts, of course. This necropolis is a bona fide curiosity here in the one-time Roman province of Sopianae, which was on the outskirts of the empire. Outside it's still dark, and inside we're in strange company. On

the walls we see Adam and Eve, the prophet Daniel among the lions, Jonah and the whale, Noah and the ark. This might be called the cradle of our thousand-year-old culture—and, of course, also its coffin.

### 06:00

On we go, this time to eastern Hungary's *puszta*, a vast area of plains and wetlands, and in particular that breathtaking part of it called the Hortobágy. We take in sunrise in the country's first and largest national park, established in 1973: Hortobágy National Park. We imagine a cowboy or, more precisely, a horseherd, galloping by. He's cracking his whip, the horses are going at full tilt. So is this what the Hungarians were like in olden times? A tranquil flock of racka sheep (see "Livestock" chapter) are grazing yonder, while a herd of grey cattle (same chapter) are resting over by that Hortobágy landmark, the nine-arched bridge. All around these livestock are the requisite dogs, herding and protecting flock and herd alike: the shaggy black Puli and its huge white counterpart, the Komondor. As the sun rises ever higher, everything seems to come alive, but we don't wait around for the scorching heat.

### 09:00

On to western Hungary, to Pannonhalma, home of Hungary's Benedictine order. The scene resembles that sublime rocky hill to the south of Rome, Monte Cassino, where St. Benedict founded his first monastery back in 529. The monastery at Pannonhalma is not quite as old, but it is old. It was established by Prince Géza and his son Stephen I, Hungary's first king and a future saint. Today's basilica was built at the beginning of the thirteenth century, and its ornamental gate, the Porta Speciosa, is also from this period. The convent's refectory and dining room are lavishly beautiful, as is its library, which houses the first contiguous Hungarian language text, the deed of the Tihany Convent from way back in 1055. Chiming farewell to the thousand-year-old stones and spiritual milieu is the noontime bell, an ever-present reminder of Hungary's landmark triumph over the Turks in 1456 at Nándorfehérvár (known today by its Serbian name, Belgrade).

### 12:00
Time to head back in the other direction, all the way to the hilly region in north-central Hungary that is home to the immaculately preserved historic village of Hollókő. The Hungarians waged plenty of battles with the Turks around here, too. This is a memento to the Hungarian people's stormy centuries: perched on a hill above the village are the ruins of a fortress, and underneath, the tiny houses comprising this once poor village of Palóc folk, a subethnic group of Magyars who inhabit much of north-central and northeastern Hungary. It is indeed a little slice of the past, with its houses reconstructed after its most recent ravaging fire, in 1908; with its revived folk customs and traditions; and with its folksy old ladies who have remained here to this day.

### 15:00
Where to now? Tokaj, of course, the most celebrated center of fine Hungarian wine—the home of Dionysus, where the Tisza and the Bodrog rivers meet. Why are Tokaj wines so special? Because they are made from grapes cultivated on a volcanic hill, grapes that grow on fertile, sun-drenched, southward facing slopes whose climate is just right—all this being highly conducive to the development of Botrytis cinerea, the "noble rot" that gives the late-harvest aszú grapes their unmistakable zest. All that's left is to pick the grapes, press out the juice, and then the aszú can ferment in nice little oak barrels in the cool cellars of Tokaj. "*Vinum regum, rex vinorum,*" it's been said of Tokaj aszú for centuries now: "The wine of kings, the king of wines." Fancy words? Yes, but anyone who has tasted this unforgettable wine can confirm that there is also substance behind them.

### 18:00
About face and right across Hungary to its northwestern corner, to the vicinity of the Lake Fertő, or Neusiedlersee by its German name

(only fair to mention, as much of it lies in Austria). This body of water is Europe's, nay, Eurasia's, largest salt lake. Over the course of its well-known history it dried up more than once, most recently in the 1860s. What makes it unique these days is not only its salty water but also the remains of bygone bogs as well as the varied fauna—not least, rich bird life—around the lake. This naturally sublime ambience is gloriously punctuated on the Hungarian side of the border by the imposing, baroque castle at nearby Fertőd—whose one-time owners, the Esterházy princes, once employed Joseph Haydn—and by the residence in Nagycenk (also nearby) of the man known as the "greatest Hungarian" of the nineteenth century or any century for that matter, István Széchenyi. At every step we are amid architecture evoking the Austro-Hungarian past common to the two countries that share this lake, memories proving increasingly important these days.

*21:00*
Finally we pull into Budapest. The city looks positively dignified in its evening light. We take a seat on the Danube-side promenade amid a spirited mass of ever-moving youth and look pensively about with the disposition of those older tourists who tread here more attentively. István Széchenyi's famous Lánchíd (Chain Bridge) is all lit up, linking hills with flatness, Roman and medieval ruins with architecture from more recent eras, wealth with poverty—Buda with Pest. The House of Parliament is a bit oversized, like a confectioner's dream cake big enough to feed one thousand or ten thousand sweet tooths. Ambling along the arrow-straight length of the city's holiest of holy grand boulevards, the Parisian-style Andrássy Street, we finally arrive at the great national pantheon: kings, princes, and revolutionary heroes commingle on this single, open public space, Heroes' Square. A thousand years of history in statues: a compact country in twenty-four hours. This, too, is world heritage—Hungary's heritage.

# capital city

Péter Rácz

It rests on the two banks of the Danube. Even the Romans inhabited this place. (But not the Greeks.) Its natural treasures: mineral waters and underground hot springs. Among its legendary thermal baths: the Gellért, the Rudas, the Király, the Termál (on Margaret Island), the Rác, and the Széchenyi. And then there is the iconic Buda Castle, which has been battled over many a time. In the sixteenth century we Hungarians made a mess of defending it, and so the Turks easily occupied it. A century-and-a-half later we managed to reoccupy it with international help. At the end of World War II, however, we would have been wiser not to defend it at all, for then Budapest might have pulled through things relatively damage-free, and its bridges would not have been blown into the Danube.

The Buda Castle, on Castle Hill, is today Hungary's citadel of culture. It is home to the National Széchényi Library, the Historical Museum, the National Gallery, and the National Archives. The Office of the President got a home here in 2003—in the imposing Sándor Palace.

As for Budapest's symbolic sites: Heroes' Square, which marks the end of Andrássy Street on the Pest side of the river; the Széchényi Chain Bridge and other bridges connecting Buda and Pest; the Fishermen's Bastion on Castle Hill; Gellért Hill, likewise in Buda; the 1896 subway (more commonly referred to as "the underground," as per British English), that runs the length of grand old Andrássy Street and beyond, right under City Park before soon reaching its terminus; the House of Parliament, occupying a sizeable stretch of river in Pest; Matthias Church (on Castle Hill by the Fishermen's Bastion); the

Basilica, which marks Pest's most imposing rooftop and is the center of Roman Catholicism in the capital; the Dohány Street Synagogue; Vörösmarty Square with its landmark coffeehouse, the Gerbeaud; the Main Food Market; Margaret Island; Andrássy Street itself, Hungary's take on the Champs-Élysées; and the Ecseri Street flea market on the outskirts of Pest. Just a few of its bygone coffeehouses, which live on in memories and in literary works: the New York, the Japán, the Hadik, and the Centrál. Of these, the Centrál reopened in the 1990s to great fanfare, and the New York Palace threw off its scaffolding in 2006 after years of renovation—reemerging in perhaps even more opulent splendor than it had to begin with, thanks to an Italian chain that also opened a luxury hotel there. And then there are other cafés and café-dotted squares and streets with a rich past that lives on: There are the Eckermann and the Művész, on Andrássy Street. Just off Andrássy Street there is Jókai Square, which is simply brimming with cafés. And, yes, there is that narrow but zestful little thoroughfare likewise in Pest, Ráday Street.

Budapest's iconic settings include (just to mention a few) its food markets and flea markets; and ever-crowded Moszkva Square, where people of all regional cultures, as well as of cultures further afield, cross paths. As for bookstores, you can't beat the Irók boltja (Writer's Shop) along Andrássy Street. Ships? If you're in a party mood, venture on over to the Buda side of the Petőfi Bridge and step aboard Ship A38, a one-time Ukrainian stone-carrying vessel that, since April 30, 2003, has enjoyed a new life as a nightspot to reckon with. And we mustn't forget about the Trafó, that hip arts and cultural center in a lately revived neighborhood of Pest many blocks away from the main center-city action, just beyond the Ring Boulevard. When it comes to being both loud and crowded, there's no beating the annual, one-week "Diák Sziget" (Student Island) Woodstock-style affair, on an island on the southern outskirts of Budapest that's jam-packed with people and popular and rock music of all sorts, day and night. (For juicy details, see the chapter, "Entertainment.")

Budapest's downtown neighborhoods were named after members

of the House of Habsburg (the suffix *város* meaning "city" when used alone as a word but "district" or "borough" in this, present-day sense): Lipótváros, Erzsébetváros, Terézváros, Józsefváros, and Ferencváros. The capital's outermost districts (Kispest, Újpest, Pestszentimre, and Csepel) officially became part of the city in the early 1950s, notably expanding its size. This greater Budapest today has around 1.7 million inhabitants, down from more than 2 million in 1990; the increased flow of capital and the construction boom after the fall of communism saw many Budapesters move to suburban towns.

Compared to some major cities of the developing world, the streets of Budapest may seem quite clean, but by the best West European standards it ostensibly aspires to, they are dirty beyond comprehension. The reason: dogs and people. Not that the two species leave behind the same sort of thing or that we're drawing a moral equivalent here; the people, to make things absolutely clear, are prone to littering and to chucking their cigarette butts all over the place, and to looking on lackadaisically as their dogs do what they must do.

Likewise "beyond comprehension" (but here in a positive sense) is Budapest's rich cultural menu. Except in summer, you have your choice of two or three events daily in each of these categories: music, theater, literature, and the visual arts. The capital's impressive network of art cinemas and all the cafés and bookstores found near them offer that much more of a cultural experience.

In the final third of the nineteenth century, Budapest suddenly took off on a course of development worthy of (and consciously modeled after) a world-class city. That's when its main transportation arteries took on their present look, and when many of the landmark buildings that today still define downtown Budapest arose; more than a few of these buildings exhibit an art nouveau style, with a certain Hungarian sensibility woven in. Although a good many of downtown Budapest's buildings were destroyed in World War II (and in 1956), by the present-day almost all such bombed out shells have been filled in—whether with a new or rebuilt building, or with a park or other public space.

So far, the economic-political sea change that ensued in 1990 hasn't yielded any truly exciting architectural developments, notwithstanding a few notable new edifices such as the National Concert Hall. The trams are still yellow, the coaches are blue, the trolleys are red. Budapest's road network is nothing to write home about; indeed, it gets worse and worse every year. The Buda side of the river is hilly, of course, whereas Pest is flat, flat, flat. Buda is home to the "better" or, at least, fancier neighborhoods, most of which are naturally named after the hills they are on: Várhegy (Castle Hill), Rózsadomb (Rose Hill), Gellérthegy (Gellért Hill), and Szabadsághegy (Liberty Hill). Meanwhile, residents of Pest can take heart that their half of the city has always been the main venue for revolutions, that life is livelier there, and that Pest is more accommodating of change.

Budapest is also a regional leader when it comes to shopping malls and entertainment centers, which have room for upwards of 100,000 consumers. Indeed, our exalted capital leads the world in time per capita spent in malls.

By contrast, bicycle paths are few and far between: Budapest residents go everywhere by car if they can afford it. That said, there are places where you can see lots of bicycles all the same, mainly at night: young and old people by the hundreds fill up alternative entertainment venues and bars in out-of-the-way neighborhoods, in otherwise empty, onetime industrial facilities or warehouses, or in parks, often until the wee hours.

Budapest is chock full of little, round-the-clock grocery stores. And this brings us right to the topic of how those who live here see their capital: It often seems as if foreigners living here—and in particular, the Chinese and Turkish shop-owners and restaurateurs who've done their fair share to build up the city's retail food sector since around 1990—not to mention those people here to study our music or language, are fonder of Budapest than are we Budapesters ourselves. This is but an illusion, however. Take it from me: the city has many a fan even among the natives.

As ethnically diverse as Budapest is, there are unofficially, subtly or not so subtly segregated pockets of the capital here and there of varying size occupied by Gypsies, Jews, Bulgarians, Armenians, Serbs, and Chinese. Since Budapest can't claim to have anything in the way of a Little Italy, though, we Hungarians ourselves see to making and eating Italian pizza and Italian ice cream.

In days past, particular trades reigned over a little corner of this or that neighborhood comprising a few streets. For example, the upholsterers held sway along Baross Street in the 8th district; the prostitutes pretty much owned Rákóczi Square a few blocks away; antiquarian bookshops were particularly fond of Múzeum körút; antique dealers occupied every other doorway on Falk Miksa Street; and Király Street was practically synonymous with second-hand electronics.

Budapest is up to its neck in traffic jams and low on subway lines and green spaces. City Park, that tranquil sweeping expanse of Pest, is a notable exception. One recent attraction at its edge is the world's largest hourglass, the Timewheel, which makes one complete rotation each year. Visitors are few and far between, though, so it's no wonder that few Budapesters can keep track of time.

Last but not least, Budapest has a good many more homeless people and beggars than apparent. This social issue is as impossible to resolve as is meting out punishment to those vandals who grace so many walls about town with unsightly bits of graffiti. (We're not talking about graffiti artists here.) In addition to those places well known to tourists, other positively atmospheric parts and pieces of town—especially on weekends, which are relatively calm—include vast reaches of the 8th and 9th districts as well as the streets of Újlipótváros and remaining historic buildings in what was, in World War II, the Jewish ghetto.

# symbol

## Ádám Masát

January 1, 2000. Quite a crowd gathered on Budapest's Kossuth Square on this day, by the Parliament Building. No, it was neither post–New Year's Eve giddiness that drove people here nor the hope of seeing fireworks over the Danube—but rather the arrival of the Holy Crown, which was being carted over from the National Museum amid plenty of pomp and circumstance. Why was moving the Crown necessary?

The Holy Crown is not only the most important symbol of Hungarian royalty, it is also one of our most important national relics and, moreover, the symbol of 1,000 years of Hungarian statehood. Why did the center-right government led by Viktor Orbán—a government popularly characterized in Hungary as having a "national-conservative" bent—decide to move the Crown on the occasion of the Millennium? In a nutshell: because, in its view, this symbol would have a more worthy home under the imposing cupola of the Parliament Building. Only days before, on December 21, 1999, Parliament approved a bill mandating the move—a piece of legislation that was roundly criticized, especially by the liberal opposition. One such minority party, the Alliance of Free Democrats, opined that although the Crown was a decisive aspect of Hungary's past (i.e., as a Christian kingdom) and a well-respected historical relic, the spirit of the Crown and the spirit of the (democratic, officially secular) Republic of Hungary—the latter as represented by the Parliament Building—were hardly compatible. This particular liberal party argued that the Crown embodied political traditions the Republic's "founding fathers" sought to break with back in 1989 as Hungary was on the verge of becoming a liberal democracy; and, moreover, that bestowing the Crown with renewed political status would weaken the principle of popular rule inherent to a democracy.

Physically speaking, the Holy Crown comprises two parts. The upper part, consisting of four arched gold bands welded together up top into a cupola-like shape, was called the *corona latina* (Latin Crown) after the Latin inscriptions accompanying its illustrations. Bearing enamel images of eight apostles and of Christ Pantokrator, this rests atop a circular, likewise gold band also featuring images, but with Greek inscriptions; these include icons of saints and of Christ Pantokrator, as well as pictures of the Hungarian king Géza (1074-1077) and the Byzantine emperor Michael VII Doukas (1071–1078). This lower part is the *corona graeca* (Greek Crown).

Although of all Hungary's royal symbols we know the most about the Holy Crown, researchers still aren't capable of reaching consensus on even the most fundamental questions. For example, they can't even agree on the Crown's origins. We know neither the precise time nor place of its making; nor do we know just why the gold cross that tops it off is attached in a slanted position—though this particular question positively enthralls most Hungarians. The clash of opinions concerning the Crown is shown vividly by the fact that there are engineers who maintain that the cross was slanted from the time of its making; and then there are goldsmiths who say that the cross once stood straight, and became slanted only later; which is not to mention those historians who contend that in 1551 Queen Izabella accidentally broke off the cross, upon which another was set crookedly in its place. Yet others blame Prince Otto of Bavaria for the cross's slant, alleging that while fleeing Hungary in 1305 after deciding he didn't really want to reign there, he lost the Crown (which he'd hidden in a gourd hung to a saddle). Although the precious relic was miraculously found a day later, supposedly it was damaged. As likely as this may seem, according to the most recent research the cross became crooked in 1638 when the case containing the Crown was forcibly opened.

Amid the lingering questions two things are, however, indisputable. First, the Holy Crown was a so-called "inauguration crown," worn by Hungary's rulers only on the occasion of their being crowned. We further know for certain that most Hungarian kings were crowned with this particular crown, which is to say that even by the most cautious estimates, the Holy Crown found its way, if briefly, to the top of at least fifty Magyar royal heads.

From the first half of the fifteenth century, the person who at any given time happened to be Hungary's ruling king increasingly took a back seat to the Crown in terms of symbolic importance. Indeed, Hungary's people began to become known as "subjects of the Holy Crown"; acquired territories were called "Countries of the Holy Crown"; in courts of law oaths had to be made not only to God and to the king but also to the Holy Crown; and even the royal treasury became the "treasury of the Holy Crown."

The nineteenth century saw the idea of the Holy Crown reinterpreted more than once: the great statesman Ferenc Deák spoke of the Crown in terms of Hungary's territorial integrity; Lajos Kossuth endeavored to bring the serfs into the fold of the Holy Crown; and, for his part, the legal historian Imre Hajnik (1840–1902) wrote in the final third of the century that the Holy Crown had become the "symbol of executive power divided between the king and the people; which is to say, of constitutional power." After the collapse of the Austro-Hungarian Monarchy the doctrine of the Holy Crown was reinterpreted yet again. The conviction that all territories once belonging to the Holy Crown were an inviolable part of the Crown became an argument in favor of the demand to reappropriate the territories Hungary lost under the Treaty of Trianon in 1920.

The Holy Crown was therefore more than simply a royal symbol, and over the course of stormy centuries it also became the most important symbol of Hungarian statehood. And so it is likewise understandable why its move to the Parliament Building should have sparked such heated debate at the turn of the millennium. The debate was not so much about where to store a national relic, but much more about the compatibility of the ideals it embodies with the spirit of the Third Hungarian Republic (i.e., post-communist Hungary). What does the Crown symbolize, and what message or meaning does it embody in the new era of democracy that ensued with the fall of a decades-long autocratic regime? In light of Hungary's tumultuous twentieth-century history, it is of course nothing short of a miracle that the Crown is still with us at all.

After the assumption of power in 1944 by the fascist Arrow Cross Party, the Crown was first taken to Veszprém, in central Hungary a few hours south of Budapest, and then to the small town of Kőszeg and the nearby village of Velem in western Hungary, on the Austrian border; and from there to the Austrian towns of Mariazell and, later, Mattsee. From there the Americans took it via Germany—Augsburg and Frankfurt, to be precise—all the way to Fort Knox in Kentucky, from where, some thirty years later, in January 1978, under President Jimmy Carter, it was finally returned to Hungary.

Over the course of its adventuresome travels the Crown has been dropped and buried more than once, and it even spent some time soaking in a swamp. After its many ups and downs, we Hungarians can be grateful that our foremost national relic did not perish. And while the question of where it is to be kept—the National Museum or the Parliament Building?—can and will certainly be argued over, what is most important is that the Crown remains in one piece for future generations.

# holiday

## Ádám Masát

All eyes were on the parliamentary debate of March 5, 1991. That was the day MPs were to decide which among Hungary's three foremost national holidays was to become *the* official state holiday: March 15, the first day of the 1848–49 revolution? August 20, the anniversary of the canonization of Hungary's first king, Stephen? Or, perhaps, October 23, the day associated not only with the 1956 revolution but also with the proclamation, in 1989, of the democratic, multiparty Republic of Hungary? It was clear to all that this was not simply a matter of establishing a hierarchy of holidays but, rather, as per established practise in other nations, of choosing one particular day that would achieve legitimacy both in Hungary and abroad as *the* official state holiday. Arguments were voiced in support of all three dates, and consensus was lacking even within the political parties represented in Parliament. Within the parties of the governing coalition—the Hungarian Democratic Forum, the Independent Smallholders Party, and the Christian Democratic People's Party—most MPs sided with August 20. The MPs in the two liberal opposition parties—the Alliance of Free Democrats and the Alliance of Young Democrats (Fidesz, since known more as a conservative party)—raised their voices forcefully in support of March 15. And, although opinions were divided within the Hungarian Socialist Party—which, also in the opposition, was most associated in the public mind with the communist regime, as many of its members had come straight from the ranks of the former Hungarian Socialist Workers Party—the party did make it known that it would not support October 23.

Why did October 23 receive the least support? The regime led by János Kádár, which took power in late 1956 and kept a firm grip for some three decades, had consistently stuck to the line that the popular uprising which took hold of Hungary in the fall of that year represented a "counterrevolution"; and not until soon before the fall of communism could this be publicly questioned without unpleasant consequences to aspiring questioners. Understandably enough, the Hungarian Socialist Party had a more difficult time of it knowing what to say about the events of 1956 than did other parties. Indeed, its predecessor, the Hungarian Socialist Workers Party, had rejected out of hand everything the 1956 "freedom fighters" (as those who supported the revolution called its most active participants) had struggled for.

As for other political parties, the main problem they saw with October 23 was that not enough time had passed by to create a sense of historical distance from those events. Indeed, after thirty-three years of silence, in the run-up to 1991 Hungary had seen a veritable eruption of varying opinions on October 1956. Even the freedom fighters themselves often remembered the events differently. What did seem in favor of October 23's ascendancy to the status of official state holiday was the fact that on that day in 1956, all eyes in the Western world were on Hungary; and, moreover, that it was on that day in 1989 that the democratic Republic of Hungary had been declared. In contrast to the other two holidays under consideration, the events of October 23 were therefore widely known abroad, and at the same time the date also marked the birth of the then still young Third Hungarian Republic.

That said, Hungary's revolution that first began manifesting the ideals of the "age of reform" began on March 15, 1848. It was on that day—without the censor's permission—that Sándor Petőfi's poem "Nemzeti dal" (National Song) and the twelve points comprising the revolution's key demands, titled *Mit kíván a magyar nemzet?* (What Does the Hungarian Nation Desire?), were printed and promulgated for all to read and hear. Among other things, the Hungarian nation desired freedom of the press, equal justice before the law, a fair sharing of the tax burden, the establishment of both a national bank and a national guard, and union with Transylvania—all of this in line with the ideals of freedom and equality as embodied by the spirit of the French Revolution.

Those MPs who, more than 150 years later, supported this particular date as Hungary's official state holiday argued that March 15 unified the nation more than any other day; that Hungary's various religious, intellectual, and political groups were more in agreement on this holiday than any other. Yet another argument in favor of this date was that during the communist era, March 15 became a symbol of the opposition: it was during mass demonstrations held every year on this day from the 1970s on that Hungarians publicly expressed their desire for freedom with perhaps the most intensity. In the public mind, then, March 15 had come to represent a link between the long-cherished ideals of national independence and the more recent social, economic, and political transformation that Hungary's adoption of a free market, multiparty democracy entailed. Indeed, it wasn't by chance that on March 15, 1989, the distinguished actor György Cserhalmi read a twelve-point proclamation in front of the Hungarian State Television building whose demands included the withdrawal of Soviet forces from Hungary; the creation of an independent, democratic Hungary; and the nation's overall political and economic transformation.

And then there was August 20, St. Stephen's Day, one of Hungary's oldest holidays. It was on this day in 1083 that Pope Gregory VII canonized Hungary's first king. The day was probably a church holiday in Hungary beginning in the reign of Lajos the Great (1342–83), and in the 1770s it was Maria Theresa who had declared it a national holiday. During the brief period of multiparty democracy right after World War II, this day was declared the "holiday of new bread." But then, only a couple of years later, the passage of a new constitution establishing the communist dictatorship of Mátyás Rákosi was deliberately timed for this day—meaning that until 1989, Hungarians were compelled officially to celebrate this day as "Constitution Day." Quite a fix. While a certain uncertainty of content therefore surrounded August 20, in sheer political terms to most MPs, the day signified the celebration of Hungarian statehood, which had commenced with Stephen's coronation in the year 1000 (possibly on Christmas Day, which would have made for an awkward national holiday in 1991). This was a key consideration as the turn of the twenty-first century neared.

Although on March 5, 1991, the parties did not reach consensus, the majority of MPs nonetheless voted for August 20. This decision showed that emphasizing Hungary's popularly conceived historical continuity proved more important that the particular range of ideals associated with each of the two revolutions also at issue. In 1989, both March 15 and October 23 had exceptionally important roles as motivating forces behind the peaceful negotiations comprising Hungary's velvet revolution; for a parallel could be drawn between the revolutionary ideals of 1848 and 1956 and the demands associated with the collapse of one-party communist rule. However, what the vote on March 5, 1991, signalled was this: Now that Hungary had jumped the hurdle and had firmly embarked on a new democratic era, it had less of a need for the two holidays marking their respective revolutions than it had had two years earlier, when the country's political-economic sea change was still very much underway.

This, then, is how August 20 became Hungary's official state holiday—a day that, unfortunately, we are compelled to celebrate when everyone from foreign diplomats to Hungarian MPs and indeed most other Hungarians (few of whom have much of an emotional attachment to this day) are away enjoying their summer vacations. At most, Hungarians—if they happen to be in Hungary, that is, rather than on some faraway beach in Croatia—hear on the news that, as every year, the evening fireworks over the Danube dazzled one and all, and St. Stephen's mummified right hand again made its way around downtown Budapest from its resting place in the Basilica.

# folk customs

## Katalin Suzuki Berkes

As is the case with major transitions in many people's lives, with the holidays on our calendars, and even with some of our everyday pursuits, religion played a decisive role in the development of Hungarian folk customs. It is, then, not by chance that the bulk of those folk customs that endure to this day in Hungary and are considered "Hungarian" or as being of folk origin can be traced back to the Counter-Reformation of the sixteenth century.

In the secularized world of the twentieth and twenty-first centuries, however, those folk customs that have lived on among broad sectors of the public—often in revised form—have done so because they managed to substitute their religious content with some other message. Such customs have stood their ground either in conjunction with, or else independent of, a religious understanding of the world. Let's take a look at two of these customs of ours that have survived to this day—customs associated with two distinct reaches of the calendar and with holidays that have special significance in Christian cultures: the Christmas and Easter periods.

Those of us who celebrate Christmas in some measure are inclined, above all, to put up a Christmas tree as this holiday draws near. We hang it with the obligatory *szaloncukor*: bite-sized chocolate covered fondants that come in a glittery Christmas wrapping. These can be bought in supermarkets in sizeable boxes in the run-up to Christmas. On Christmas Eve we sit down for a festive supper, after which we exchange gifts. And whether or not we also commemorate the birth of Jesus, we regard this occasion to be, more than any other holiday, woven through with a sense of family togetherness and of love. The same evening, by the tree, we sing—or at least listen to a recording of—Hungary's most popular Christmas song, *Mennyből az angyal* (Angel from Heaven). Our Christmas gifts are slipped into our homes neither by Father Christmas nor by Father Winter through the chimney or the window, but—so those Hungarian kids are told who are raised in families with a sense of piety toward Christ and/or their Christian cultural heritage—by none other than *Jézuska* (Baby Jesus) himself, who places them under the tree, perhaps beside a nativity scene.

The Christmas tree—the modern-day manifestation of the "fruit-bearing" evergreen bough (aka "Tree of Life") hung in bygone days symbolically from the main girder beam of a home—became widespread in Hungary from the late-nineteenth century on, initially among the bourgeois and, later, in village homes, under the influence of a corresponding German and Austrian custom.

The previously mentioned ornamental, delectable candy called *szaloncukor* was the product of the turn-of-the-twentieth-century Hungarian bourgeois world; and this explains its Hungarian name: *szalon* (salon) *cukor* (candy). It is known to all Hungarians who hold the Christmas tree dear. Yet another, traditional aspect of this candy was is its leaf-thin aluminum foil wrapping. At first the candy itself was homemade, and eventually it became a sought-after factory-made product, flavored with cocoa or walnut. Today it comes in all sorts of artificial flavors and often takes the form not of a fondant, but of a thick jelly within its outer coating of chocolate. (In its most traditional form and flavors, at least, it is a bona fide Hungarian speciality that no Magyar with a sweet tooth and a nostalgia for the Christmas tradition can resist!) No less sweet or at least conducive to a really special, intimate atmosphere were the predecessors of *szaloncukor* that graced the table on Christmas Eve: a red apple; some other fruit; and, yes, popcorn.

The generally meatless nature of the foods traditionally consumed in Hungary on Christmas Eve endures to this day, more or less: bean soup, fish, poppy-seed and walnut brioches, and walnut rolls. The presence of sweets rich with walnuts and poppy seeds on Christmas Eve suggests fruitfulness and fertility—even if we tend to forget such symbolism nowadays.

That which was formerly the duty of godparents, and then parents, toward their children today applies to everyone: Christmas is a holiday of giving and receiving gifts. As for our extraordinary wealth of lovely Christmas carols, which varied by denomination and had their roots in that nebulous realm where folk customs and religious practice overlap, it's not the living tradition it once was; for we Hungarians have long shown a predilection for accommodating ourselves to European and American musical traditions.

On to that illustrious springtime holiday, Easter. This is when—so folk custom has it, anyway—girls and women paint eggs, whether in one or many colors. And in exchange for having their heads sprinkled with eau de toilette on Easter Monday by tradition-minded boys and men, they might give the sprinkling male a bit of money, a shot of *pálinka* or a glass of wine, or a slice or two of pastry. This is the case in a tradition minded village, at least; in a town or city the playful male is more likely than not to come away with but a smile or a kiss.

These days few boys and men head to the well to fetch water for the sprinkling, but instead all the more of them go buy themselves a little bottle of toilet water, whose fragrant drops they sprinkle on the heads of girls and women while reciting a light little poem that generally draws a parallel between femininity and fruitfulness; for example, the words might suggest that the female being sprinkled upon is a flower—a flower that, with a bit of water (or toilet water) can be expected to grow even lovelier.

For Hungarians, Easter Monday has remained the day of customs relatively removed from explicit religious content—indeed, it was a bank holiday even in the communist era—whereas the three days comprising Good Friday through Easter Sunday continue to be set aside for expressions of Easter's religious significance.

On those Easter days many Hungarians embellish their homes with a bit of holiday ornamentation. They might put a pussy-willow branch in a vase, which they then surround with painted eggs or with store-bought, chocolate versions shaped like sheep and rabbits. Much as with walnuts and poppy seeds at Christmastime, the rabbit found its way into Easter traditions as a fertility symbol. In Hungary, it arrived at the end of the nineteenth century under German influence.

The Easter bunny enjoys huge popularity these days: it "lays" the red Easter egg and it single-handedly hides little gifts for children in gardens and in secret places at home. And, although in some countryside homes rabbits are slaughtered and then feasted upon to celebrate Easter, our more common sacrificial foods at Easter include smoked ham with horseradish sauce and boiled eggs. In some regions, local traditions continue to support special Easter foods; for example, sweet curd prepared with eggs, a tradition in parts of northern and northeastern Hungary.

As for Easter songs, they've all but vanished from the customs practiced by most Hungarians during this holiday. This is in part because such songs embody purely religious themes, and in part because they have long melded with folklore-rooted texts that either convey a wish of general welfare or request donations, a tradition practiced only in a few places these days. Then again, this leaves all the more room to nurture—true, on Easter Monday—the lovely tradition of "sprinkling verse"!

# folk dancing

## Ádám Masát

If we ask a foreigner if she has ever heard about Hungarian dancing, in all probability she will mention the common name of our couples dance, the csárdás (pronounced "chahr-dahsh"). However, this would presumably be little more than a geographic categorization: Just as many people associate the bolero and the flamenco with Spain, the jig and the reel with Ireland, and the waltz and the landler with Austria, so they associate the csárdás—*Tschardasch* as the Germans call it—with Hungary. These days, even Hungarians themselves tend to know little of substance about their most popular national dance; indeed, what they do know can be summed up in ten words (only six in Hungarian, mind you): "Two steps to the right, two steps to the left."

And yet the csárdás and Hungarian folk dancing in general represent an incredibly rich cultural heritage, as rediscovered by the *táncház* (dance hall) movement that blossomed in the 1970s—which, as its name suggests, established folk dance centers across Hungary. The sheer wealth of motifs embodied in the dances, and especially in the csárdás, lives on to this day; even how couples hold each other differs by region and by figure. This movement led many Hungarians to realize that not only do costumes and music vary by region, but that each region also has its particular store of dances. The dance culture developed and preserved over generations by Hungary's peasantry differed from place to place, and although there were plenty of identical elements—such as the well-known circular turn couples make in the csárdás; the turning of the female under the male's arm; and the technique by which the female, following the male's lead, steps swiftly halfway around him, and in the process switches from holding one of his hands to holding the·other—the figures were rendered in different styles and methods in practically every region of the country.

Let us then take a quick look at the different types of Hungarian folk dances, so as to illustrate their wealth of diversity.

There are three main regional "dialects" of Hungarian dance: those of the Danube region (the Danube running north to south right down the center of Hungary and also along its northwest border), which embraces much of western Hungary; those of the Tisza region, the Tisza river likewise flowing generally north to south, but through eastern Hungary; and those of Transylvania even more to the east, situated in present-day Romania.

As for historic development, we can talk in terms of old and new styles of dance. Among the older dances there are *botolók* (stick dances), which preserve traces of weapons dances, and other *eszközös* dances (those featuring implements); *karikázók* (round dances) performed and sung by women in southern Transdanubia (i.e., that part of southern Hungary lying west of the Danube) and in northeastern Hungary; and, last but not least, both the *ugrós* (jumping) dances still widespread in today's Hungary and the virtuoso men's dances native to Transylvania that are commonly called *legényesek* (lad's dances).

Hungary's new-style dances comprise the *verbunk* (recruitment dance) and the csárdás, which emerged beginning in the early nineteenth century. The various forms of the verbunk that survive to this day are danced by men, either solo or else as a circular group. As for the csárdás, two main types of varying tempo survive, more or less: the *lassú* (slow) csárdás and the *friss* (rapid) csárdás. The csárdás in particular was that dance in the reform era of the first half of the nineteenth century which, in a form adapted slightly from a couples dance prevalent among the peasantry, managed to break its way onto the ballrooms of the nobility and the bourgeoisie. Thus, it was not by chance that it quickly became known among the upper classes even in neighboring countries, and indeed it became so popular that by century's end practically all other Hungarian dances were relegated to the shadows. The csárdás had become our nation's preeminent couples dance.

In contrast with the more fixed-form couples dances known in Western Europe, the csárdás was a fiery, blood-blazing, improvisational dance from its birth. Indeed, this bestowed the couple—and in particular the man, who led—with freedom; and this seemingly trivial sense of liberation meant a lot in an era when the ideas of the French Enlightenment were reaching Hungary, and ever more people were yearning for liberty and national independence as a refreshing alternative to oppression. And so the csárdás came to reinforce national consciousness, symbolically expressing Hungarians' endeavors against the Habsburgs—that is, in the language of dance. Another factor in the growing popularity of the csárdás was the music that accompanied it, which ranged from new-fashioned folk songs and folksy, freshly composed songs to ever popular Gypsy music.

The year 1999 saw the international premiere of the Budapest Dance Ensemble's production "Csárdás! Tango of the East," which has been a huge success ever since. If we go back in thought for a moment to the age of reform and equate the East with Eastern Europe, which undeniably lagged behind Western Europe in terms of development, then comparing the csárdás with the tango seems quite appropriate. The csárdás spread like wildfire after its initial emergence: It became a determining presence in the dance culture of the Carpathian Basin; it fulfilled a symbolic role in the cultural, intellectual, and political awakening that marked the age of reform; and the entire Hungarian nation came to consider this dance its own. True, the csárdás never did become as popular internationally as the tango, and most Hungarian young people today are more familiar with the tango—which, however, we Hungarians might call, with just a bit of bias, mind you, the "Latin csárdás."

# folk costumes

Katalin Suzuki Berkes

As with so many other facets of Hungarian culture, the nation's folk costumes long stood at the crossroads of influences from East and West. Even apart from geographic, economic, and social factors, general types of clothing can be found in a great many regional varieties, and certain items of attire—such as wide, bell-bottomed, white linen trousers, round sheepskin cloaks, boots, embroidered mantles, sheepskin jackets, and even kerchiefs—took on a distinctive Hungarian look both in the eyes of foreigners and of the Hungarians themselves.

For example, at the end of the eighteenth century, boots assumed a "Magyar" style in Hungary precisely because they incorporated Western influences on a form that was essentially Turkish. And, with its straight, rectangular patterns, the embroidered mantle—which became the symbol of the free citizens of the western city of Debrecen at the end of the nineteenth century—preserves an Eastern form, which is again exactly why we consider it Hungarian.

In short, folk costumes derived their distinctive "Magyar" look primarily from the method of their making and from the meticulous attention devoted to fine details of design. However, all this came to be emphasized only from the age of Romanticism.

In addition to expressing social status and rank, peasant costumes were also charged with precisely representing gender, age, and family status. Amid the prevailing fashions of our contemporary age, however, folk costumes have a different role. With their traditional functions on the wane, folk costumes (or elements thereof) may well carry different connotations when we see them worn about town or village. Say we're in downtown Budapest and spot a woman decked out in a colorful folk costume; a woman who, we are certain, is an ethnic Hungarian from the Transylvanian village of Szék—a village that has nothing much to do with the Székely region elsewhere in Transylvania, but which is where a good many such folk-costume-adorned ladies on the streets of Budapest happen to be from. She is in traditional garb from head to toe: a red-and-white kerchief, a broad skirt with red-and-black stripes, and so on. No matter how many fine details might reveal her social status, we immediately think one thing: she is dressed this way here in our cosmopolitan capital precisely because she is bent on selling folk embroideries to passers-by.

What comes to mind when we glimpse a plump little old lady in the vicinity of the East Railway Station wearing a short, black linen skirt, a dark kerchief, and a pack-basket on her back? Hardly do we think of how many family members she might be mourning, or which village of Palóc people in northern Hungary she hails from— assuming the latter occurs to us at all. Instead we're apt to wonder if the chicken eggs in that basket of hers (for we assume there must be eggs in there) are fresher than those in the corner fruit-and-vegetable shop, and whether her raspberries are less pricey.

When we see a young person in the city running across the street with a woven satchel at his or her side, we know at once that he or she is not taking victuals to the reapers toiling away out on the field, but is most likely headed to a folk dancing center.

And what comes to mind if we happen to be walking along downtown Budapest's main pedestrian thoroughfare, Váci Street, and can't help but notice someone coming toward us wearing an embroidered shirt straight out of the *puszta*—whether in the Kalocsa style characteristic of the south or that of the Matyó people more to the north? Why, we immediately suspect that this person is a foreigner, and if he or she asks for directions, we obligingly relate how they can get to the "Central Market" just down the street, whose second floor is chock full of folklore-related gifts, and where they can choose to their heart's delight from among made-for-the-market, ready-made clothes; clothes that, at most, are manufactured by specialists in the particular folk motif they purport to reflect.

The case is the same with those who wear folk costumes by profession, from musicians to dancers to other performers in the various folklore-related events that take place every day across Hungary. While it can be safely presumed that these people don't identify wholly with their occasional dress—which carries the weight of sundry symbolic functions, after all—some sort of conscious identification with what they have on is nonetheless suggested by the very fact that they're wearing it in public.

That said, even these days there are places and situations in Hungary, and among Hungarians more broadly, in which the wearers of such clothing can identify completely with what they have on. For example, this is the  case among the oldest generation of people in the easternmost group of ethnic Magyars of all, the Csángó people of Moldavia (a region in eastern Romania). There, the *katrinca* or *lepelszoknya*—a woven rectangular skirt that opens in front and has a pinned-up left edge—still has clout. (This skirt also occurs among neighboring ethnic Romanians.) Another common sight among these people even today is a (likewise homemade) linen shirt with embroidered shoulders—as is walking barefoot. All in all, such dress (or the lack thereof, when barefoot) signifies not some sort of romantic symbol but, more likely, economic necessity.

Among Transylvania's Székely Hungarians and a few other distinct groups of ethnic Magyars (most of them likewise from Transylvania), the folk costumes they don for special holidays still convey important messages about not only one's age group or a family's social status but also one's particular ethnic-cum-local identity. Indeed, these are communities of ethnic Magyars that, for historical reasons, continue to harbor an enhanced sense of regional identity—as compared, for example, with most contemporary Hungarians from Hungary proper. In Transylvania, they hail either from the Székely Land (Hung. Székelyföld) or, say, from the Kalotaszeg region west of the cultural capital of Kolozsvár (Cluj-Napoca, Romania); the Torockó region southwest of Kolozsvár; or the large, mildly hilly Mezőség region of central Transylvania.

The folk costume designs in use today are hardly more than a century old. Indeed, it is roughly to the end of the nineteenth century that we can date a process still underway, if sporadically; a process Hungarian researchers call *kivetkôzés* or "divesting." This process has seen peasant attire and folk costumes gradually vanish from the realm of everyday, mainstream fashion. Before disappearing completely, however, they have incorporated more variety and color than ever before—from blue-dyed calico to silk and velvet, brocades, and various supplemental adornments that can be made from colored beads and ribbons. This is due to an abundant selection of increasingly low-cost, factory-made textiles, ornaments, and dye. In Hungary, as more and more peasant folk acquired the economic resources to make such new-fashioned costumes for themselves—from relatively expensive materials and dyes that could not be produced at home, that is—the more they awoke to differences in wealth and status even among themselves, and, indeed, to their own potential in society.

# folk music

## Katalin Suzuki Berkes

Discussing the musical culture of Hungary—the native land of Béla
Bartók (1881–1945) and Zoltán Kodály (1882–1967)—is impossible
without first reflecting on the "discovery" of folk music and the inten-
sifying efforts to collect it at the turn of the twentieth century. That's
not to mention today's continuing endeavors to seek new ways of
articulating and expressing folk music motifs.

The present-day popularity of Hungarian folk music can be
traced back largely to a movement that gathered steam in the
1970s to establish folk dancing centers nationwide. The *táncház*
(dance hall) movement revived not only Budapest's cultural life but
also those rural communities to which attention was cast. Its most
striking success was represented by the musical and dance traditions
associated with the village of Szék, in Transylvania's Mezőség region.
Remarkably, this tradition was transplanted virtually intact from
the "dance halls" of this village to the cultural centers of Budapest,
which were chock full of young intellectuals and students; indeed, the
very notion of the *táncház*, so ubiquitous in Hungary today, derives
from this tradition. As an alternative means of entertainment, the
*táncház* movement spurred both the re-establishment of folk music
groups that used authentic instruments and a burgeoning number of
folk music adaptations that sought a return to the roots. Traditions
of verse and minstrelsy that could be coupled with folk music also
gained new vigor. True, the Hungarian *nóta* (popular song), which
had long been misidentified with Hungarian folk music, never did go
out of fashion over the twentieth century. In fact, this style of music
derived not from folk music but from composed contemporary

music, including Gypsy music by professional Gypsy musicians. Such music had yet other offshoots, but those are even more distant from folk music in the traditional sense.

What, then, characterizes Hungary's authentic folk music tradition as reflected by the oldest available recordings? When Bartók and other collectors first took to the countryside with recording equipment at the outset of the twentieth century, Bartók complained that practically every which way he went, he heard only "new-style" songs. This trend had indeed taken firm shape by the late-nineteenth century in the form of innumerable, vastly popular newfangled melodies that drew on everything from dance songs (especially for the csárdás) to military songs. By the early twentieth century, in line with trends elsewhere in Europe, such new-style songs had largely cast more authentic, "old style" Hungarian folk music into the shadows. Still, dedicated collectors did manage to unearth an old-style tradition of folk song lyrics that varied by region and embodied a rich history, as well as a wealth of themes and functions.

Among Hungary's oldest musical traditions is that of free-structure, recitative melodies whose roots stretch back to the Ugric period (i.e., well before the Magyars occupied the Carpathian Basin from the east, in 896)—melodies preserved in laments sung in the context of mourning rituals. Similarly archaic are those folk songs for children that comprise both narrow-range tunes and songs with only a few notes. As for the pentatonic tunes within the realm of Hungarian folk music, they represent a Eurasian tradition, and this is reinforced and enriched by Old Turkic musical influence. The bulk of old-style Hungarian folk songs comprise pentatonic and, especially, descending strophic (often fifth-shifting) tunes.

Western European influence appeared in the wake of the Magyars' occupation of the Carpathian Basin, adding yet another touch of color to the world of old-style Hungarian folk music—as time passed, in the realms of both church and secular music.

Finally, by the eighteenth and nineteenth centuries, there came into fashion a store of folk and dance music that assimilated the traditions of classical Viennese music—namely, the *verbunkos* (recruitment song). This represented a transitional phase between the old and new styles of Hungarian folk music. Notwithstanding its foreign influence, the verbunkos fit smoothly into our nation's earlier musical traditions; indeed, it bears close relation to *kanásztánc* (swineherds' dance) and *ugrós tánc* (jumping dance) melodies. It remained popular even as old-style folk music began to wane. This marked the first time in Hungary that the music of the peasantry and the nobility came within close proximity of each other. Paradoxically, the verbunkos, despite its origins from beyond our nation's cultural borders, is yet another characteristic slice of our musical tradition that non-Hungarians typically associate with Hungarian folk music.

Hungarian folk songs are almost invariably monophonic—that is, they have a single melodic line—and in this respect they differ in character from the folk songs of the neighboring Slavic peoples. That said, alongside folk songs per se, Hungarian folk music also comprises polyphonic instrumental works; these are, however, usually accompanied by lyrics. While *purely* instrumental music makes up a comparatively small slice of our nation's folk music, the popularity of Hungarian folk music has ironically long been sustained for the most part by solely instrumental groups; for such groups, which comprise chiefly string instruments, are most adept at catering to the musical tastes of the masses. Indeed, ever since Hungary's modern-day folk music movement took off in the 1970s, instrumental groups have played a key role in credibly conveying the nation's folk music traditions.

# language

## Orsolya Nádor

"Difficult!"—snaps Hungarian and non-Hungarian alike on being asked for their take on the Magyar tongue. But isn't every language difficult, especially when you set yourself the task of learning words and grammar by rote? It's at least as trying for Hungarians to learn any language decently as it is for native speakers of other languages to tackle the wonderful world of Hungarian—with its definite and indefinite inflection, verb prefixes, distinctive word order; and, yes, words that appear unrelated to any other language. That said, non-Hungarians have been trying to learn our language ever since the first Christian missionaries landed among us—and if we consider that Hungarians became Christian, after all, this initial phase of Hungarian language learning could not have been a failure. The missionaries were followed by many thousands more who learned Hungarian either within Hungary itself or in some other country.

So then, we've resolved one of the main obstacles to learning Hungarian: the notion that it can't be learned. It can! Let us now consider the other main facts, facets, and figures of our lovely language.

Hungarian—as regards the number of its speakers—occupies a relatively illustrious position among the world's several thousand languages, ranging between fortieth and forty-second. There are almost 15 million native speakers of the language, not including the many thousands who learned the language at universities and language schools in other countries and, indeed, in Hungary. Although we Hungarians are proud that so many folks out there are interested in our curiosity of a language, we cannot help but be painfully aware that Hungarian is still among the world's lesser known and lesser taught languages.

Hungarian vocabulary mirrors Hungarian history. If we examine the origins of our words, a picture emerges before us of the many peoples and cultures the Magyars encountered in the course of their nomadic centuries, followed by their settlement in the Carpathian Basin and the 1,100-plus years since. Also apparent are the various ways in which Hungarian culture was enriched by these "encounters" (which of course include longer and shorter periods of willing or unwilling cohabitation).

Most loan words in Hungarian found their way into our language—along with attendant cultural practices or traditions—from Slavic languages, Latin, and German. As is the case with so many other languages in recent decades, English loan words have more recently been the most prominent among those appearing in Hungarian. Such words have generally accommodated themselves to the overall logic of our language, taking on prefixes and suffixes to the point where discerning with any certainty just where they came from is all but impossible. Take, for example, *alma* (apple—of Turkic origin), *selejt* (dregs, castoffs—from German), and *fotel* (armchair—from French) as well as our many Slavic words including *asztal* (table), *udvar* (yard), *málna* (raspberry), and *péntek* (Friday).

Hungarian grammar is extremely logical, say some; it is anything but, others contend. One striking singularity of our language is its capacity to mould and mutate words—with the help of prefixes, signs, and suffixes—to the point of being unrecognizable. However, word order imposes limits on this seemingly boundless creativity: by attaching a suffix to the end of a word, we close off the opportunity for further changes. Based on its mode of inflection, linguists categorize Hungarian as an *agglutinative* language.

A comparison of Hungarian with the most widely known Indo-European languages reveals numerous aspects of the former that are unknown in English, German, Italian, and so on. And vice-versa: there are plenty of linguistic features in the latter family of languages that are absent from Hungarian. Let's look at some examples.

One striking, unintentionally PC singularity of Hungarian is its gender-neutral pronoun "ő." To Hungarians, in this respect, at least, "he" = "she" = "it." Students of the language are exasperated to no end, however, by verbal inflection based on whether an object is definite or indefinite. Although word order in Hungarian appears rather free from an Indo-European perspective—and indeed this misimpression is the source of numerous errors—every Hungarian child knows full well that a given question can be followed only by a reply with a given word order. If the word order changes, the reply answers *not* the question that was asked but another question!

Yet another bit of phonetic wizardry on the part of Hungarian involves its often subtle distinction between long and short vowels and consonants. To cite just one example in which this hinges on the difference between a simple umlaut-adorned *ö* and a long, double-acute-accent adorned *ő*: *megörül* (to rejoice) versus *megőrül* (to go mad). In Hungarian, it's not enough to learn a suffix, because most have two forms, and sometimes you'll even encounter three—this being where the language's obligatory vowel harmony comes into play.

Students of Hungarian typically consider the connections between expressions of space and time as among the language's logical singularities; and the same goes for the three-directional word grouping of *hol* (where), *honnan* (from where), and *hova* (to where). However, students have a tough time of it when it comes to the imperative. This is due not only to phonetic challenges such as various forms of assimilation (*adja ide*: give it to me), but to the fact that in reported speech (the conjunctive) we use the same verb form even though we are not calling upon anyone to do anything. We have no single verb *to have*, but in consequence what we do have—namely, *van* (*to be* or *to have*)—fulfils two tasks: it expresses both being and possession. However, we have two means of expressing the plural: there is the simple suffix *k*, which signals merely that there is more than one of something; and then there is the suffix *i*, which means that a person can own more than one of a thing. For example, someone can have *könyvei* (his/her books).

Speaking of "his her," this bit of clumsiness in English isn't clumsy at all in Hungarian, which is singularly gender-neutral in this respect—as manifested in the third-person pronoun *ő*.

Finally, there is something about the Hungarian language that makes it unique in Eastern Europe: a third of its native speakers live *not* in present-day Hungary but either within the fold of an ethnic minority in a neighboring country or else scattered throughout the world. Wherever a Hungarian is born or raised, however, he or she will understand a fellow Hungarian speaker from even the most distant corner of the world; while the language does have its dialects, the differences between them are sufficient only to bestow the speaker with local color, but without posing an obstacle to comprehension.

"A nation lives in its language." Hungarians often cite this saying from the age of Romanticism. Indeed, for centuries now they've been consciously tracking the development of their precious language, looking after it, scolding it, nurturing it, and defending it. To Hungarians, even in the twenty-first century their mother tongue shapes and maintains their national identity more than anything else.

Original text of the *Halotti beszéd* (Funeral Oration), the earliest existing Hungarian text written in the Latin alphabet (between 1191 and 1195).

# literature

## Péter Rácz

It's secretive. Our cloistered language, which seems so cryptic or exotic from afar, is the veil that conceals it from those outside; for this language is precisely its medium of expression. *It* is, of course, our literature. "Go ahead, read it!" says language coquettishly before turning up its nose and adding, "Learn me first, or else you can't possibly have an inkling as to what it's all about."

Say you *do* manage, after all, to learn some of this language's essential verse. You might begin with that celebrated adage from the first Hungarian poetic record, *Ómagyar Mária-siralom* (Old Hungarian Lament of the Holy Virgin, c. 1300): "*Világ világa / Virágnak virága / Keservesen kínoznak / Vas szegekkel átvernek!*" (Light of the World / Flower of Flowers / Cruelly art Thou tortured / And pierced with iron nails!*). From there you could move on to Dániel Berzsenyi's (1776–1836) lyric agonizing over his fellow Hungarians. How about Mihály Vörösmarty's (1800–55) piercing cosmic vision in *Előszó* (Preface)? Or Sándor Petőfi's (1823–49) aching sentiments for his love, for his beloved Hungarian landscape or, of course, for the cause of Hungarian freedom? A few poems by two early-twentieth-century greats, Endre Ady (1877–1919) and Attila József (1905–37) might also resonate in your ears. Even given all this, however, can you truly *feel* what it all means for us, the Hungarians? Not unless you've lived here for ten or twenty years and have read, read, and re-read it all.

Practically every Hungarian schoolchild is a walking repository of poems by the above-mentioned figures. They recognize them at once even if they've actually heard only a fraction of them. And yet these poets and their works represent but a fraction of the landmarks of

* Translated by Michael Beevor, p. 30 of *In Quest of the "Miracle Stag": The Poetry of Hungary.* Ed. Adam Makkai. Chicago: Atlantis-Centaur, 1996.

Hungarian literature! Every Hungarian knows a couple of dozen lines from Gáspár Károli's revered translation of the Bible (1590) without so much as knowing where they're quoting from. Not only has János Arany's (1817–83) trilogy *Toldi* endured for well over a hundred years without going stale, but so too has his monumental transla-tion of Shakespeare, which Hungarians regard as every bit as beautiful in Hungarian, and quite possibly even more so, than it is in English. Kálmán Mikszáth (1847–1910) penned prose; Mór Jókai (1825–1904) wrote historical novels; Gyula Krúdy (1878–1933) churned out stories and novels that created an entire imaginative universe with the romantic gentleman-protagonist Szindbád at its center; and Zsigmond Móricz (1879–1942) dabbled in all of the above.

Yes, all this, too, is today inseparable from the very notion of being Hungarian, of *Hungarianness*. And then I haven't even mentioned Dezső Kosztolányi (1885–1936), who excelled at fiction and poetry alike; or Sándor Márai (1900–89),who, although he spent his final decades living in virtual anonymity in California, is today regarded as among Hungary's—and Europe's—twentieth-century literary lions. No, no, I haven't forgotten the others, but there's not room enough to list even all our favorites. Every Hungarian knows the children's verse of Sándor Weöres (1913–89), many of us know yet more of his resonant lines. And it's impossible to read even the spare verse of János Pilinszky (1921–81) without being moved to the very fabric of your being. The romantic and political poems of György Petri (1943–2000) comprise a typifying and vigorous impression of the era he lived in.

Meanwhile, the literature of present-day Hungary—the mother country, that is—is enriched by ethnic Hungarian writers who hail from neighboring countries (which, prior to 1920, were part of Hungary) and in many cases have settled down in Hungary. There is, for example, the verse of Ottó Tolnai (1940), who represents the enduring literary vitality of the Magyars in Serbia's province of Vojvodina. And then there is the surrealism-inclined prose of Ádám Bodor (1936), which nurtures our sense of the mystery and immensity of Transylvania. The poetry and prose of Dezső Tandori (1938) represents a response to private life and politics alike with its palpitating undercurrents and penchant for formal experimentation.

Perhaps it's easiest these days for non-Hungarians to cozy up to the prose of Péter Nádas (1942) and Péter Esterházy (1950), seeing as how both have been translated into numerous languages. But is it possible to know the essence behind even their writing, really? Just as many answers emerge to this question as there are readers of Hungarian literature. Literature, its creators, and its readers inhabit one language. Anyone with a sense of the richness of our language can likewise have a sense of the sheer exuberance of our literature.

In Hungary, poets and writers have for centuries pointed the way for "the people." The poet in particular has risen to the task of articulating the nation's past and the future—and, sometimes, the present—and the writer has often done so as well. These days, thank goodness, poets are expected only to produce poetry when they sit down in front of a blank sheet of paper. When Hungarian novelist Imre Kertész (1929) won the Nobel Prize for Literature in 2002, many Hungarians thought, justifiably enough: finally! True, Hungarian literature has another two or three nominees it would like to see up there with Kertész in the next few years.

Hungary is also home to a well-established if often overlooked tradition of literature by women and, less visibly, of "women's literature." Magda Szabó (1917–2007), the most canonized Hungarian woman writer of the twentieth century, is the best example of the former, though in some of her novels she treated personal themes and was perhaps the first major Hungarian woman writer to broach the subject of women's sexuality. Zsuzsa Rakovszky, who has lately excelled as a novelist after establishing her name as one of the naton's finest poets, is among today's most prominent writers. As for women's literature, although writing by women about women existed in Hungary long ago, too, less attention was devoted to it back then—one prominent exception being Margit

Kaffka (1880–1918), whose autobiographical novels mined the problem of women's changing roles in modern society and earned the respect of her male contemporaries.

And, yes, literature translated into Hungarian from other languages has always had a profound role in Hungarian literature. The twentieth century in particular saw a great deal of prose and poetry given new life in Hungarian, often by the most exceptional writers and poets. And so it is no wonder, perhaps, that the classic works of world literature exist in the Hungarian collective consciousness virtually as if they were written in Hungarian. Meanwhile, the translation of Hungarian literature to other languages has gathered force in recent years through the support of such institutions as the Hungarian Translators House Foundation (www.forditohaz.hu).

So then, dear reader, do you *really* see into the Hungarian soul, the Hungarian universe, the Hungarian language, if, on some rainy afternoon or else under a lamp one evening, you chance to open a Hungarian book, whether in Hungarian or in translation? No, impossible! But do seize the day, anyway—delight in those sentences as they unfold, delight in the stories you're told.

# contemporary writer

## Szabolcs Parragh

More likely than not, the contemporary Hungarian writer is churning out his or her product for the German market. Even if this isn't consciously the case, it's quite probable that he or she (henceforth *he*, both for simplicity's sake and because most prominent examples that come to mind happen to be men) is writing a story set in Berlin or, perhaps, an early modern German tale; or, yes, a novel that recounts many generations in the life of a Jewish family. Of course, bringing this off is a hard task for a Hungarian writer, seeing as how he is writing in Hungarian, and the Hungarian language is anything but German. That's the best-case scenario. And that is why the reader back home in Hungary is impossible to avoid. That reader is, after all, the one with whom the writer shares a mother tongue.

The contemporary Hungarian writer inhabits a small country, to be sure, but the forest of words in which he feels at home is large indeed. And so this writer seeks to lure those few readers who read him in the original language, and who also understand what it is he has written, into this forest of Hungarian words. (We're generally talking a few hundred or a few thousand readers, by the way.) Reality is rather a distraction in this writer's work. As a professional literary artist, he shies away from politics. As a public figure, on the other hand, sometimes this writer does indeed jump on the bandwagon by signing some petition or otherwise joining up with a cause. And so the contemporary Hungarian writer's relationship with reality is ambivalent, we might say.

The said writer isn't terribly interested in money, and so can rarely be found pouting over this. By ancestry he might be aristocratic or the descendant of an apparatchik, the scion of a working class family, or the latest in a long line of bourgeois intellectuals. Variety is the rule. Regardless of origins, however, the contemporary Hungarian writer generally knows his way around the past; for indeed this writer—assuming he is at least well into his twenties, that is—inhabited this past for a greater or lesser degree of time. As a result, this writer is a bit flustered, too, for the past can sometimes seem real indeed.

Let us take, for example, the contemporary writer whose oeuvre represents the greatest source of trepidation for the student of Hungarian who lives abroad or has come to Hungary. This writer is a bona fide count. Indeed, he's an Esterházy. Péter. The now-twenty-first-century scion of one of the most important families in Hungarian history. And so Péter Esterházy is the living past incarnate, as he himself points out in his novel *Harmonia Caelestis* (Celestial Harmony), published in Hungary in 2000 (and in English, in America and elsewhere, a couple of years later). This is a book the critic can praise and the reader can understand. It is a magisterial experiment with memory and with the past, which in the end are transformed into language, into words. The protagonist of this linguistic universe is (as Esterházy calls him) *"édesapám"* (literally: *my dear father*), who is simultaneously the writer's real, flesh-and-blood father; the collective father comprising all fathers of the Esterházy family; and, indeed, anyone and everyone from the past who lives within us (i.e., within the writer and his readers).

The sequel to this novel—which concerns the utter collapse of the memorial Esterházy constructed for this father in the previous novel—is by contrast more of a contemporary Hungarian story. Sadly, reality intervened for Péter Esterházy when it turned out (around the time of the earlier novel's publication) that his father (alas, the flesh-and-blood variety) had been an informer for the secret police during the communist era. The writer, who made this discovery himself while poring over declassified state archives, saw fit to then publish a "corrected edition" to the previous book, an extended afterword of sorts he aptly named *Javított kiadás* (Corrected Edition). This appeared in Hungary in 2002. In this book, then, he confronts the relentless force of reality. This confrontation brings him fear, tears, and bitterness. And it has flustered more than a few expert readers, too, who had just begun to take solace from the fact that literature had finally lost its direct relationship with reality. No such luck: The unrelenting vindictiveness of the real world again linked literature and reality. Yes, that all-too familiar feeling returned: we were reading a book that addresses the reader who lives *here*, among *us*, in today's Hungary, less than two decades after the fall of communism. Not that this sensation was completely unexpected: our domestic media has long been serving up a regular, juicy menu of news about everyone who, it turns out, was a secret police informer in those dark days—which singer, writer, government minister, journalist, and so on.

In short, *Corrected Edition* became a best-seller in Hungary—one we could find even on supermarket shelves, nay, in the checkout aisle, right beside the ubiquitous gummy candy and disposable razors.

The contemporary Hungarian writer is, then, a poor wretch stuck between language and reality. He struggles through one nation's monumental transition from totalitarianism to democracy—a task for which he builds a literary and thus linguistic hinterland. (See Esterházy's monumental and exceedingly playful *Bevezetés a szépirodalomba* [Introduction to Literature] and his essays likewise written when the communist regime was on the wane.) He believes that the world is one big text, and that the universal metaphor for life is play. But reality reins him in again and again. So it is that literature once more becomes a mirror, one by which—even if a bit dimly and distortedly—we see ourselves.

Of course there are contemporary Hungarian writers to whom all this doesn't apply. But, no, that's not the sort of writer we were talking about here.

# poets

## Péter Rácz

Impassioned, private, self-sacrificing, and agonizing over the fate of his homeland and the world—this is what comes to mind when we think of Sándor Petőfi (1823–49), the most famous Hungarian poet in the world. His short life made room for everything we might expect of a Romantic poet. His poems are easy to quote from, whether in full or in part; indeed, in Hungary more than a few such quotes have become adages. But let's go a bit further back in time for a couple of sentences. If a Hungarian poet is to be remembered, being a warrior and knowing how to handle a sword can't hurt, nay, such traits lend one's verse a crucial bit of credibility. Bálint Balassi (1554–94) and Miklós Zrínyi (1620–64) are two illustrious examples. Expressly fretting over the fate of Hungarians is yet another poetic task, with Ferenc Kölcsey (1790–1838) and Mihály Vörösmarty (1800–55) among those who best knew how to do so. By the second half of the nineteenth century, not only did Hungary's poets begin looking more bourgeois but some even had jobs; indeed, some were gainfully employed by the Academy of Sciences, as was János Arany (1817–82). A fiery temper, revelry, and an unstable livelihood are traits as particular to our poets as is a predilection toward prophet-hood, with Endre Ady (1877–1919) the undisputed master on this front.

Above all, the Hungarian poet is supposed to suffer, be unhappy, and shoulder the burden of his homeland's troubles and worries—and of course he is obliged to write all this down. Indeed, he is tasked with articulating "for others" what everyone feels.

Ensuing from his profession, the good poet must sometimes bear with the admiration of his female devotees, but the better poets rise up to this task, too. (This is assuming that he is a man, of course; but with some notable twentieth- and twenty-first century exceptions, tradition has until now generally seen to it that this has been the case.) The poet is self-educated and indeed educated (or not). For the sake of making a living, he's a lawyer or, say, a newspaperman, and as such he lives a debauched life and lugs himself along from one day to the next. In short, he is not considered a man of stable means. Fathers fear for their daughters in his presence. It is his task to whip his people into consciousness when they're sluggish, slavish, and uncultured. And, assuming he doesn't "cast his watchful eyes on Paris"—as did poet János Batsányi in his 1789 work "Changes in France," in which he warned all tyrants to cast their watchful eyes in that direction—why then, he might even be overly optimistic or pessimistic, as has been the charge of Hungarian poets for centuries now. The Magyar poet not only peers into the depths of the soul but is also sometimes the engineer of the soul; and what he experiences fills him with horror, as was the case with Attila József (1905–37), who so famously ended his misery in the path of a train.

The poet is not exactly a family man. (Again, this is assuming he's a man; while the iconic image of "the poet" as it lives even today in most Hungarian minds is still mostly male, in recent decades ever more women have been staking their claims in this exalted territory.) And if a man with a family harbors such ambitions, let's just say his family isn't overjoyed. Since he draws his bow along the strings of emotion, he has an enhanced need for love; for women, that is. The individual who serves as the poet's muse is, in the poet's telling, capable of anything and everything; the poet Lőrinc Szabó (1900–57) told us this, at any rate.

The poet may be committed as regards his political or social sympathies, which he sometimes proclaims for all the world to read and or hear, though such endeavors rarely meet with success. And so it's best if he remains uncommitted. Posterity will either understand or forget lesser excesses, and the present-day will endure them. In the worst-case scenario, it is the poet's task to give answers to life's big questions; in the best-case scenario, to ask the questions to begin with.

Since poets do ask a whole lot of questions (and in this respect they resemble children), there has developed (in Hungarian) the concept of the *költôi kérdés*, which translates literally into English as "poetic question" but more recognizably as "rhetorical question." This is a question that requires no answer. Poets are sharp observers; indeed, this is an occupational hazard they share with prose writers. That which they observe, they describe in words.

In the absence of a feel for form, you get prose; otherwise a poem might be born. Naturally a poet is not obliged to tell the truth. No, all he must watch out for is not to be caught red-handed when lying. That said, he can write anything at all, for he can distance himself comfortably from the authorial "I."

Seeing as how poetry is taken seriously in Hungary, the poet is not just anyone. There was a time when he was more important than even the king. So too, we have had working class, nay, outright proletarian poets, who, unlike bourgeois and decadent poets, did not have the option of ensconcing themselves in the proverbial ivory tower. No, such poets were compelled to draw their themes from the stuff of real life.

Just a few among Hungary's still living or lately late, great modern-day poets whose reputations have remained intact over the decades include Zsófia Balla, György Faludi, Ágnes Gergely, Sándor Kányádi, Ágnes Nemes-Nagy, János Pilinszky, György Petri, Dezső Tándori, Imre Oravecz, Ottó Orbán, Ottó Tolnai, and Zsuzsa Rakovszky.

That which is exalted, lofty, and sublime was once typically called "poetic." Today the poet is dry, austere, and understylized. Indeed, the contemporary Hungarian poet is no more important than anyone else. He or she is simply a private individual—an individual whose lot it is to tinker and or struggle with our lovely language.

# painters

Adrienn Szentesi

The early 1800s saw the establishment in Bavaria of the Munich Academy, which made quite a name for itself in the second half of the century as the single most influential school of painting in Central and Eastern Europe. Among the Hungarian artists who created their works within its walls were Mihály Munkácsy, József Rippl-Rónai, and Tivadar Csontváry Kosztka. All three also spent time in Paris, the capital of art and painting in that era. They had something else in common, too: they are widely regarded as the greatest Hungarian painters of all.

Mihály Munkácsy (1844–1900) began his career by painting romantic scenes, then he tried his hand at *en plein air* (in the open air) landscapes, and he was further influenced by historical academicism. One of his most famous works, *Siralomház* (Cell of the Condemned), won a gold medal at the Paris Salon, which was the real measure of every self-respecting painter of the era. Only the bona fide greats made it into the Salon.

Munkácsy became the champion, teacher, and patron of the Hungarian artists in Paris. Between 1870 and 1880 he produced primarily genre paintings, landscapes, and portraits, the more famous among these being *Tépéscsinálók* (Making Lint, 1871) and *Leány a kútnál* (Girl at the Well, 1874). The telltale signs of romanticism are also evident in *Rôzsehordó nô*⊠ (Woman Gathering Brushwood, 1873). From the late 1870s until his death, his art was characterized by monumental paintings born in the spirit of academicism. This period also saw his justifiably most famous body of work, the so-called *Munkácsy Trilogy*, comprising

*Krisztus Pilátus elôtt* (Christ Before Pilate, 1881), *Golgota* (Golgotha, 1883), and *Ecce Homo* (1895–96). These three paintings simultaneously manifest Renaissance, classical, and realist modes of visual depiction. Since 1995, the trilogy has been on display in the Déri Museum (www.derimuz.hu) in the city of Debrecen, eastern Hungary, although only Ecce Homo is under Hungarian ownership.

Just why did Munkácsy become one of our most important painters? Because he had a remarkable feel for color and form, which he allowed to unfold for themselves; and because he arrived at the realization that capturing the essence of "silence" is sometimes more important than capturing grand events. What he immortalized, above all, were the silences.

A native of the small city of Kaposvár in southwest Hungary, József Rippl-Rónai (1861–1927) was one of Munkácsy's many students, but their paths soon diverged. Rippl-Rónai left his master because he was interested in trying his hand at practically everything—which is to say, at all the prevailing Western styles of his era. His canvases record his relationship with his surroundings, which enchanted him again and again. His first successes were small-scale portraits of women; for example, *Nô⊠ fehér pettyes ruhában* (Woman in a White-Spotted Dress, 1889) and *Kalitkás nô* (Woman with a Cage, 1892). The latter work is one of his greatest, and it is characteristic of his time in Paris, of the "black" period by which his oeuvre is readily distinguishable from those of his contemporaries.

Those painters of the era who are today considered most emblematic of their times were influenced above all by the French art nouveau; by the expressive force of colors and by dynamic contours. Thus it should come as no surprise that in 1899 Rippl-Rónai spent three months in Banyuls-sur-Mer, France. The Pyrenean landscape and the view of the sea had a profound effect on him; so much so, that his "black" period came to an end: restrained colors appeared on his paintings from this point on, as did a new approach to three-dimensional representation. The proof of the pudding was his work *Aristide Maillol portréja* (Portrait of Aristide Maillol, 1899), which is exhibited in the Musée d'Orsay in Paris.

In 1902 Rippl-Rónai returned to Kaposvár, where the intimate circumstances of being back in his hometown again gave his paintings new life. From this point on his works were to reveal a particularly sensitive relationship to the world, a lyrical romanticism. Rippl-Rónai approached the people around him with empathy. His most famous work from this period is *Piacsek bácsi babákkal* (Uncle Piacsek with Dolls, 1905), in which the colors positively sparkle and space has expanded. By then, Rippl-Rónai was recognized even in Hungary; his paintings were in demand, and he became a famous and wealthy man. The key identifying trait of his final period consists of "spotted" brushstrokes. His works were rich with emphatic contours, thick lines, and spots placed roughly side-by-side, the foreground marked by intellect and pure logic. The chalk portraits of his final years do justice to the personalities they depict, including those he did in 1923 of the celebrated literary artists Mihály Babits, Zsigmond Móricz, and Lőrinc Szabó. In addition to painting, Rippl-Rónai also designed tapestry, glassware, and ceramics. On this front, his most famous piece is a tapestry he made for the dining room wall of Count Gyula Andrássy's household, a work titled *Piros ruhás nő* (Woman in a Red Dress).

It is no exaggeration to say that Tivadar Csontváry Kosztka (1853–1919) was very much in a class of his own. He was neither a great master nor a virtuoso stylist. His art was a singular phenomenon; there has been no such body of work before or since. He worked with beautiful albeit extravagant colors that well outdid reality, and his travels to exotic lands had a profound effect on his already strange style. Csontváry painted for but fifteen years in all, and he didn't sign his works. This has made researching his oeuvre a difficult task. Critics categorized him as belonging to the naive school, and indeed more than a few critics held him to be "half-witted" or outright insane. And yet his life was essentially a search for a "grand theme." He was benevolent, humane, and too well-intentioned for his own good. He was an odd duck to be sure. In two of his works from 1901, *Holdtölte Taorminában* (Full Moon in Taormina) and *Mandulavirágzás Taorminában* (Flowering Almonds in Taormina), which he produced at the height of his artistic powers, he seems concerned above all with the problem of light. In Csontváry's paintings, the micro world is always there beside the macro world. Fine details can be discerned on his paintings that aren't even evident at first glance; for example, the women working in the fields in the foreground of *Selmecbánya* (1902). In 1903 Csontváry painted one of his most famous works, *Római híd Mostarban* (Roman Bridge in Mostar), which is characterized by a dual perspective: the town itself has a desolate, lifeless look, and yet the bright, velvety colors, the pellucid green water, takes us into the artist's dream world. Beginning in 1903 he embarked on a tour of Europe that soon turned into a journey beyond the continent's borders, to Egypt and then the Holy Land. The blinding sunlight Csontváry experienced in the Middle East notably impacted his art. In 1907 he produced two great works. In one, *Zarándoklás a cédrusokhoz Libanonban* (Pilgrimage to the Cedars in Lebanon), the cycle of life is represented by people on horseback together with dancing female fairies under a towering cedar. Of this cycle Csontváry observed, in typical fashion that might leave one wondering just what he meant, "The light is alive, the colors are alive, but the air exists." The other, *Magányos cédrus* (Solitary Cedar), symbolizes solitude through its depiction of a lone cedar—a tree thousands of years old that links earth and sky. In this painting, the colors virtually leap right out of the canvas.

Csontváry's second last work, *Mária kútja Názáretben* (The Well of Mary in Nazareth), was not only one of his finest paintings but also encapsulated his artistic concerns perhaps more than any other. In the last ten years of his life he no longer painted; only partial outlines and various writings have remained from this period.

This, then, was where the oeuvre of Tivadar Csontváry Kosztka, the most exciting and unique character in all of Hungarian painting, drew to a close.

# paintings

## Adrienn Szentesi

*Authoritative.* Ádám Mányoki (1673–1757) spent most of his life working as a court portrait painter. In 1708 he painted his most famous work, *II. Rákóczi Ferenc arcképe* (Portrait of Ferenc Rákóczi II), which posterity considers the authoritative likeness of the legendary prince who led Hungary's freedom struggles of that era. Dark hues, most notably brown and black, predominate in this work. Light is concentrated on the prince's face, and Rákóczi's stare and his mouth convey contrasting feelings. A certain roguishness can be discerned in his brown eyes, while his lips suggest firmness and determination.

*Tragic.* In 1859, Viktor Madarász (1830–1917), the great painter of Hungary's national romantic era, produced *Hunyadi László siratása* (Lamentation over László Hunyadi), which captured the gold medal at the Paris Salon. Dark hues carry sway in this scantly lit scene. The upshot: our attention is drawn all the more to the brightly lit corpse that lies amid an otherwise dark background. The bier is simple: there are only two candles beside the body, which lies practically on the ground. The shroud is eerie in effect, as the contours of the dead man's face can be discerned underneath. And, although the mourner is in the background, this figure nonetheless casts a deep impression on the viewer of this painting.

*Depressing.* Mihály Munkácsy's (1844–1900) first masterpiece was *Siralomház* (Cell of the Condemned). Fifteen human figures can be seen in this painting, people to whom, it is safe to presume, something terrible has happened. Dark hues, not least various shades of brown and black, have the run of this painting, too; and of course this serves to reinforce the work's depressing theme. Also discernible, however, is just a bit of white and red; for example, a little girl calls attention to herself as she stands in a corner in a red skirt. What has she just been through? What fate awaits her?

*Youthful, spring-like.* Pál Szinyei Merse (1845–1920) painted his way straight into the history books of Hungarian art with his 1873 masterpiece *Majális* (Picnic in May). Hungary's only major impressionist, he was the nation's first painter to consistently take the impressionists' *en plein air* approach. With its vivid colors and mode of representation, *Majális* embodied the impressionist perspective on nature as have few other such works. The painting depicts a picnic of the sort that was typical in the art circles of Munich at that time. Central to this work is not so much the picnic per se but, rather, the perfect harmony between man and nature. Viewers of this painting are dizzied by the immortalized, capricious movements of the human figures lying about on the grassy hillside, the youthful verve and optimism by which they blend perfectly into the springtime landscape.

*Colossal.* Árpád Feszty (1856–1914) painted his iconic cyclorama, *Magyarok bejövetele* (Arrival of the Magyars, 1889), for a one-of-a-kind national celebration, the 1,000th anniversary in 1896 of the Magyars' occupation of the Carpathian Basin. Adhering to the tradition of similar panoramic paintings elsewhere in Europe, this is a monumental work indeed, at 120 meters (390 feet) long and 15 meters (49 feet) wide—which adds up to 1,800 square meters (more than 19,000 square feet). True, Feszty had the help of several of his contemporaries, including László Mednyánszky (1852–1919), who was famous for his dramatic genre paintings and landscapes. Feszty's cyclorama depicts key scenes out of Hungarian history, with transitional motifs between them. Today it is the main attraction at the National Memorial Park in the village of Ópusztaszer, on the great plain of southeastern Hungary.

*Somber.* József Rippl-Rónai (1861–1927) painted one of the most noteworthy paintings of his Parisian "black" period in 1892,

*Kalitkás nô*☒ (Woman with a Cage). Although he approached colors sensitively, as evident from many of his extraordinary works, it was nonetheless this particular melancholic painting that was to become his most famous. The work features a dark-haired woman in a dark, brownish-blackish dress and a black hat who is holding a dark green cage in her hand; in his cage we see a tiny yellow bird. The background is deep blue and green; the woman's face and dress alike are woeful and puritan. The collusion of somberness and elegant simplicity fills every point of this extraordinary work.

*Secretive.* Károly Ferenczy (1862–1917), who was among a group of important Hungarian artists schooled at the famous Nagybánya artists colony (in what is today Baia Mare, Romania), took a decidedly *en plein air* approach. His most famous work is *Október* (1903). As magnificently evident here, a particularly salient motif of his paintings is the sun, which he depicted in an entirely new way: the sun enhances the play of colors, bestowing it with an unmistakable force and resplendence. The colors in *Október* really do shine. The yellow parasol, the yellow hat, the white shirt, and the white tablecloth that are all elements of this work exude a dazzling, almost blinding glare. And yet all this light serves to veil something before us, a mystery: the secretive figure of a man, half in the sun and half in a shadow.

*Stormy.* It's not by chance that *Magányos cédrus* (Solitary Cedar, 1907) is Tivadar Csontváry Kosztka's (1853–1919) most celebrated work. This dynamic painting practically pulsates with energy. The cedar stands alone, and yet it seems to extend its reach over the entire world; it is rooted deep in the earth, but it stretches right up into the sky. It seems subject to the constant whims of a storm; we can virtually feel it being torn at by the wind. Its branches cut a strange, humanlike figure, which forcefully clutches the tree—the painting's only point of certainty. In short, forces of nature here do battle with human emotions.

*Dynamic.* Victor Vasarely (1908–97), who spent most of his life in France, was born in Pécs, southern Hungary, under the name Győző (i.e., Victor) Vásárhelyi. After devoting years to figurative, abstract forms he turned toward op-art and kinetic art. A characteristic and well-known work of his is *Zebrák* (Zebras, 1939), which depicts two zebras as they fuse perfectly, in singular, abstract form, as a single body. The black-white colors of this zebra are dazzling, and the attendant optical effects bring the entire work to life. In fact, the painting comprises only black stripes, the white background in between imparting the composition with a singular dynamic.

*Disquieting.* István Nádler (1938–), a member of the legendary avant-garde generation of the 1960s and a worthy successor of Hungarian constructivism, is one of the most important figures in contemporary Hungarian art. His work is characterized thematically by paying homage to those who have influenced his artistic path, with *Hommage à Malevics* (1985), which honors the early-twentieth-century Russian geometric abstract artist Kazimir Malevich, being an exceptional example. Stylistically, this piece is marked by geometric lines and vivid colors that give the impression of being in a frozen landscape that has just begun to thaw—and by cubes, boulders, a dissolving green, and a whirlwind that seizes everything in its path.

*Magányos cédrus* (Solitary Cedar), Tivadar Csontváry Kosztka (1853–1919)

# classical music

## Orsolya Nádor

The roots of Hungarian classical music stretch back in part to the folk traditions of pre-Christian culture, and in part to various trends of vocal and instrumental music from other parts of Europe. Although early Magyar folk songs mark the beginnings of our nation's musical traditions, in the wake of statehood in the year 1000—once Christianity and its attendant traditions conquered the Magyars' pagan culture—Gregorian chants, which could be heard in monasteries and schools, became a predominant influence. As for written records attesting to early Hungarian music, they include codices containing scores; for example, the Nádor codex from the year 1508, which preserved Hungarian-language Gregorian chants.

In addition to church music and folk music, other factors in the shaping of Hungarian classical music included our nation's medieval secular music—represented by the historical verse-chronicles of sixteenth-century minstrels whose lyrics were accompanied by violins or lutes—as well as the favorite dance music of Europe in the same period, the *Ungaresca*. The latter was based on melodies produced by the *duda* bagpipes that accompanied Hajdú dances (recruiting dances named after the Hajdú foot soldiers in Hungary's seventeenth-century wars of liberation). *Ungaresca* dance music is related to the *verbunkos* tradition, which developed from seventeenth-century military recruiting tunes. Non-Hungarians typically regard this sort of melody, whose crackling rhythm invites the listener to dance, as "Hungarian" music. This is not by chance: celebrated performing artists of the age—such as János Bihari (1764–1827), who traveled

Hungary with his five-member Gypsy band—carved out no little success for themselves by pursuing an independent genre of music, which saw this lively music—music that tickled the feet to dance—conveyed by way of virtuoso violin-playing.

The popular melodies of the *verbunkos* later found their way into numerous musical works with Hungarian themes or motifs. Indeed, the *verbunkos* bestowed even the nineteenth-century Hungarian National Opera with one of its characteristic musical motifs.

With the Baroque period, there ensued in Hungary, as elsewhere, the age of music-loving, wealthy patrons of the arts. Important works were thus born in the palaces of Hungarian aristocrats, who were happy to host the celebrated musical artists of their age and were inclined to employ entire orchestras to this end. Among the most famous such center was the Esterházy family's palace in Kismarton, northwest Hungary, where Joseph Haydn spent years as a court musician. This, too, is where Pál Esterházy composed *Harmonia Caelestis*, his work comprising no less than fifty-five cantatas, which was published there in 1711 and which is considered a milestone in Hungarian musical history. (See the chapter "Contemporary Writer" to read all about the novel of the same title, published in the year 2000 by Péter Esterházy, a contemporary scion of the same family.)

The Romantic age got underway with the emergence of Ferenc Liszt (1811–86), who will always be known by his Hungarian name in his beloved native land, but whom the outside world knows as Franz Liszt. After beginning his career as a virtuoso pianist, Liszt went on to compose a wide range of piano works—from short compositions to concertos—as well as symphonies and masses. Among the most important are, inarguably, the *Hungarian Rhapsodies* (not least: *Hungarian Rhapsody II*, from 1847), which have long tested the mettle of even the most accomplished of pianists. Foreign composers presiding over concerts in Hungary often opt for the orchestral version when giving an encore.

Opera likewise emerged from the spirit of national romanticism, and in Hungary this meant the music of Ferenc Erkel (1810–93), who composed numerous Hungarian-language operas concerning central events and personalities from the pages of our nation's history. True, only two of these operas—*Bánk bán* and *Hunyadi László*—were to prove lasting. It was likewise Erkel who set Ferenc Kölcsey's poem *Himnusz* (Anthem) to music, which gave Hungary its national anthem. This can be heard in recorded form as a choral piece, or as an orchestral rendition, at practically every festive occasion in Hungary.

Many modern-day Hungarians know a few choruses and arias from our most notable historical operas inside and out, and are given to singing them in groups (when an opportune moment of good cheer presents itself) or else just humming them alone.

A bona fide Hungarian-language night at the opera is inconceivable without the *Bordal* (Drinking Song) or the *Hazám, hazám* aria from *Bánk bán*; or else the chorus from *Hunyadi László*, which begins, "The villain has died." Erkel's art was indeed inseparable from the very notion of what it is to be Hungarian, for he drew his themes from Hungarian history, and a bit of background knowledge is necessary to understand his operas. This goes largely to explain why Verdi operas—which have often been compared to his, for they do share much in common, musically speaking—are world famous, whereas Erkel's works have remained within the framework of Hungarian culture: Verdi's themes are understandable to most everyone, while the same can't be said of Erkel's.

Beyond the fact that Erkel lived and worked in the same era of musical history as Liszt, their careers converged on Hungary's musical pedagogical scene: Erkel initiated the establishment of the Hungarian Academy of Music, whose first director was none other than Liszt. Erkel carried out most of the work, though; for not only did he teach but, during Liszt's frequent absences, he also directed the institution day-to-day.

While Magyar motifs and the musical traditions of the

common folk did find their way into nineteenth-century works of Hungarian classical music, only with the oeuvre of Hungary's great twentieth-century classical composer, Béla Bartók (1881–1945), were they subjected to full-fledged, sweeping reinterpretation. Like Liszt, Bartók was an exceptional pianist. In addition, though, his academic work earned him membership in the Hungarian Academy of Sciences (1935). True, he landed upon his unmistakable, idiosyncratic style only when he managed to part with the influence of Brahms, Wagner, Liszt, and Richard Strauss. "Only from a pure source," said Bartók, who familiarized himself with the living folk music of the Hungarian, Slavic, and Romanian peoples of the Carpathian Basin during the course of the extended collecting tours he began in 1905. He used such musical relics he acquired in two ways when composing solo instrumental and orchestral works: Either the folk music source appeared emphatically, in the center of the work (e.g., *Este a székelyeknél*— Evening at the Székelys), or else it emerges only as a motif, as for example in those works that best express his disharmonious world of sound and rhythm (e.g., *Divertimento, Concerto*).

In addition to his choral work *Psalmus Hungaricus*, which debuted in 1923, Bartók's contemporary, Zoltán Kodály (1882–1967) became world famous for the system of musical instruction he developed and grounded on folk songs and solmisation. In his 1939 essay "*Mi a magyar a zenében?*" (What's Hungarian about Music?), he writes: "We've known Hungarian or Hungarian-like music for hardly 100–150 years, and we have yet to draw a uniform picture of the Hungarian character from our history. Thus, unearthing the connections between the Hungarian character and Hungarian music is no easy task. We do, however, have a fixed point of certainty, and this happens to be in music; and we can stand on it when asking, 'What's Hungarian about Music?'" This fixed point is folk music, and, indeed, its most ancient known stratum.

Hungarian classical music of the second half of the twentieth century also bears out all of the above. Whether the works of Zsolt

Durkó (1934–97), including his oratorio *Halotti Beszéd* (Funeral Oration, 1975) and his piano and violin concertos; the harried, anguished mood characterizing the music of György Kurtág (1926), including choral works composed to accompany Hungarian poems; or the operas of Sándor Szokolay (1931)—all these have nourished themselves from this "pure source," while at the same time also assimilating the innovative techniques, melodies, and harmonies of modern music.

## Himnusz

Score of *Himnusz* (Anthem), Ferenc Kölcsey's poem set to music by Ferenc Erkel

# light music

## Adrienn Szentesi

The standard dictionary of the Hungarian language defines *könnyűzene* (light music) as follows: "Entertaining music that requires neither significant musical erudition nor immersion in listening." Even if we don't quite agree, let us stick with this convenient if facile definition. As for the "light" music you might hear in Hungary today or have heard in the past, we're talking about anything from world music and Gypsy music to cabaret, dance tunes of bygone days, and, of course, pop, rock, and their sundry variations.

"Gypsy music" is an integral aspect of Hungarian musical culture. It embodies a rich past, and it is a bona fide thread in the fabric of being Hungarian, an essential element of *Hungarianhood*.

Gypsy musicians have been a noted presence in Hungary since the end of the fifteenth century. By the eighteenth century their numbers had grown, and Gypsy musicians were regarded as the authoritative representatives of traditional Hungarian instrumental music. By the twentieth century every larger municipality in Hungary had its own respected Gypsy band; and the *primás*, the band leader, was invariably a popular figure, nay, a star—with names such as Pista Dankó and Béla Magyari etched in the mind of every Hungarian even today.

In the first half of the twentieth century, and even during communism until soon before that system's collapse, one indispensable accoutrement of any Hungarian restaurant that lay claim to ambience was a violinist well-practiced at leaning over tables and playing guests' favorite tunes. A leading man of Hungarian films of the 1930s and 1940s, Pál Jávor, invariably washed away his romantic woes with regular doses of Gypsy music. Béla Berkes, a member of one of Hungary's most famous Gypsy musical dynasties, says of Gypsy music: "A real Gypsy knows his guests impeccably. A doctor heals the body, a Gypsy heals the soul." This was in fact the case; it wasn't by chance that some Gypsy musicians became celebrities. For a long time, the most noted female singer to accompany Gypsy music was Apollónia Kovács, who in the 1960s was succeeded by Margit Bangó, who as of this writing is still singing famously away. Hungary's celebrated 100-member Gypsy Orchestra has been around since 1985, when (nearly) one hundred Gypsy musicians who gathered at the funeral of the legendary Gypsy band leader Sándor Jároka decided to establish a full-fledged concert orchestra. Many of its members graduated from Budapest's Academy of Music or another music conservatory.

While still on the subject of Gypsy music, we must not forget to mention the names of other noted Gypsy musicians and bands familiar to every Hungarian, whether Sándor Lakatos and Déki Lakatos; Kálmán Balogh's still popular Gypsy Cimbalom Band, which performs frequently (and is named after the cimbalom, a dulcimer-like instrument that figures prominently alongside the violin and double bass in any self-respecting Gypsy band); the group Andro Drom, which plays authentic Gypsy folk music; the world-famous Lakatos brothers (the virtuoso violinist Roby Lakatos, who masterfully fuses authentic Gypsy music with jazz; and Tony Lakatos, the great jazz saxophonist); and countless talented Gypsy jazz musicians.

Cabaret songs and folksy-popular dance tunes today occupy only the periphery of Hungary's light music scene, but in the first half of the twentieth century these were indisputably the country's most popular sources of musical entertainment. The great dance-tune singers of the 1940s and 1950s were real stars: Lehel Németh, Tivadar Bilicsi, Erzsi Kovács, and Stefi Ákos. In the 1960s and 1970s, they were followed by János Koós, László Aradszky, and László Komár. Their hit songs are known even today by every Hungarian.

As in many another country, the Beat era arrived in Hungary in

1962. One and all learned to make music, to play the guitar; the youth of Hungary was on the rage. This was veritable freedom worship: young Magyars wanted to listen to, and to play, Western European music; they rebelled against their parents in the spirit of free love. "You think we forgive you for everything, all the time; you think we give up every dream of ours so fine."—so sang the era's most popular Beat group, Illés. The two other most famous bands of this era included Metro and Omega, complemented by the solo starlets Sarolta Zalatnay, Kati Kovács, and Zsuzsa Koncz.

In 1967 a new era of progressive rock got underway with the founding of various bands that took scandalous music (and accompanying scandalous lifestyles) to new heights: Liversing; Dogs; Meteor; Sakkmatt (Check-Mate); Tűzkerék (Wheel of Fire); and Kex (both cute *and* salacious, as it means "biscuit" while being but one Hungarian consonant, *sz*, away from being "Szex"), with that eternal rebel, János Baksa-Soós, at its head. Their young members and fans represented the political ideals of the new left, and indeed by now theirs was a high-stakes rebellion: they wanted change. They were seeking both their past and their future; they were bent on taking on the regime in power.

In 1971 Gábor Presser founded Locomotiv GT, whose high-standard music and professional grounding might even have earned his band world fame, had political borders not meant one big roadblock. In the 1970s and 1980s groups representing even lighter, more frivolous musical fare, Hungária and Neoton Família, carved out vast popularity for themselves, and new rock bands sprang up at the same time—EDDA Művek (EDDA Works), whose singular pun of a name derived from a simultaneous allusion to both Norse literature and Hungary's industrial landscape; Beatrice; Dinamit (Dynamite); and Új Skorpió (i.e., New Scorpion). This period also heralded the arrival on Hungary's light music scene of the *csövesek* (bums, hobos), whose participants and devotees alike represented the newest forms of rebellion.

In the 1980s punk and art-punk bands emerged with a new musical style, with the former—Auróra Cirkáló (Aurora Cruiser), CPg

Csoport (CPg Group)—representing crude, deviant behavior; and the latter—URH, Kontroll Csoport, Európa Kiadó, and Bizottság—conveying more specific social criticism. These bands openly and directly confronted the communist regime. (*"Nyilvántartanak, nyilván tartanak tôled,"* sang Kontroll Csoport; that is, albeit sadly without a pun in English translation, "They have a file on you, they're clearly scared of you.") However, in contrast with the bands of the Beat era, these new groups did not rebel against the nation's musical traditions; to the contrary, alongside rock they also drew on numerous motifs of Hungarian folk music.

The 1990s brought a change to Hungary's light music scene: protests ceased, music became free. All the newfound freedom meant a death knell to alternative rock; it seemed there was no longer anyone to rebel against and no reason to rebel in the first place.

The spectrum of genres has broadened, meanwhile: groups and solo artists have emerged specializing in everything from blues, jazz, pop, rock, hard rock, metal, and hard-core to folk music and world music. Electronic music has also gained ground in Hungary in recent years, quite a few variations having developed: techno, rave, drum and bass, easy listening, jazz'n bass, soul'n bass, electro, breakbeat, and so on. Bands representing these trends are mushrooming.

Indeed, today's palate is so broad and colorful that it's hard to point to any group or any individual in particular as embodying the spirit of Hungary's light music scene in the 1990s and at the dawn of the twentieth-first century. These days, music fans can and most certainly do live by the maxim: to each his own.

# operetta

## Nóra Csontos

*Hajmási Péter, Hajmási Pál!* This pair of names—family name (pronounced *Huy-mah-shee*) first, of course, as part and parcel of being truly Hungarian—could belong to two real Hungarian brothers, but it doesn't. (At least probably not.) Those who follow the world of Hungarian operetta—and, indeed, all Hungarians—know these two names and the buoyant melody by which they're sung. But most of us have no idea whom these names really belong to, not to mention which operetta. But that doesn't matter here. We are partial to operetta not so much for the story but much rather for the music, for the spectacle that unfolds on stage. Yes, that's why we watch, listen, and enjoy operetta. *If* we enjoy it. The truth of the matter is, operetta is no longer in such fashion in Hungary as it was during its golden age, at the turn of the twentieth century.

What is classical Hungarian operetta all about, anyway? Well, its story line is simple enough: a beautiful but lonely woman—or, as termed in the operetta world, the primadonna—yearns for her love. On a moonlit night she wonders "if there will come a prince indeed, on a white steed." These princes—or, as they're called in operetta, leading men—do indeed arrive, and just as invariably they verily ignite with love. They break out in song repeatedly, finally capturing the woman's heart. Following some minor complications, tempestuous dances, and the singing of several dozen operetta hits, they become each other's and live happily ever after until death do they . . . And while the loving couples are busy trying to win each other's hearts, that other archetypal pair—the soubrette and the comic dancer—wage battle for each other and for others, too.

Hungarian operetta lived its golden age at the turn of the twentieth century. A veritable product of Austro-Hungarian cohabitation, it features lyrics that amalgamate Hungarian and Austrian vernacular speech, and music that blends the Viennese waltz and the teary-cheery world of sound characteristic of Hungarian popular songs of that time. As Béla Bartók aptly said of this operetta tradition, it is a truly Central European musical jargon.

In view of its themes and its characters, Hungarian operetta can be divided into two categories. The first comprises the "grand operetta," whose action unfolds within the ranks of the upper classes and whose characters are most often counts and countesses. It is characterized by a classic realm of sound and visual imagery; in this respect, above all, the influence of Austrian operetta is discernible. These operettas are rococo works, as it were.

The second category, that of the true "Hungarian" operetta, is a product of the early twentieth century. It features the distinctive places, everyday people, and everyday realities of the early twentieth century. Here, the primadonna is a poor, simple gal, often a secretary, who is secretly in love with a comely, inaccessible young man. One day all becomes clear: the gal lets down her bundled hair and casts aside her glasses, and the phenomenal fellow finally notices her, nay, all at once he himself falls head over heels in love! A Cinderella story of sorts. The world of visual imagery and music characteristic of the grand operetta is pushed to the background: the characters sing less often and the setting is not as glittery, but it possess an ambience of its own, a bona fide Budapest ambience.

Hungary's most famous operettas were born of the pens of such celebrated composers as Pál Ábrahám (1892–1960), Jenő Huszka (1875–1960), Mihály Eisemann (1898–1966), and Imre Kálmán (1882–1953).

The titles of these works speak volumes about the world of Hungarian operetta. There are, on the one hand, the history- and nobility-steeped titles of grand operettas—from *Gül baba*, *Prince Bob*, and *Baroness Lili* to *Countess Marica*. And then there is the unmistakably more plebian world of the "Budapest" operettas, from *My Kid Brother and I, A Kiss and Nothing Else, Kissing Woman,* and *Csárdás Queen* to those bearing common names, including *Péter Fekete* (*Peter Black*) and *Mágnás Miska* (*Miska the Magnate*).

Imre Kálmán (1882–1953)

Imre Kálmán's *Csárdás Queen*—which, Hungarians like to imagine, is still world famous—includes such songs as the justifiably perennial favorites *Te rongyos élet* (You Miserable Life) and, yes, *Hajmási Péter és Hajmási Pál*. The piece, which debuted first in Vienna (1915) and then in Budapest (1916), and was performed during World War I even in countries on the other side of the trenches, embraces everything essential about Hungarian operetta: relationships that span the class divide; hopeless but oh so promising love; humor; and, yes, music and dancing aplenty.

# composers

## Jolán Mann

"In heart and soul I am a Magyar . . . and with my musical talent I wish to serve my Hungarian homeland," Franz Liszt (1811–86) once declared. Known as *Liszt Ferenc* to Hungarians, this Hungarian of German descent was the first internationally celebrated figure in the history of Hungarian music. His works, which were often imbued with Hungarian motifs, found their way into the national consciousness.

It was his 1846 visit to Hungary that spurred Liszt to begin writing the *Hungarian Rhapsodies* (I–XV, 1851–53) and the first version of *Pest Carnival*, which later became *Hungarian Rhapsody* IX. In the course of his travels in the region Liszt took notes in a conscious effort to collect musical sources for a planned but never completed "Hungarian musical epic." His multilayered and mutually reciprocal ties to Hungarian culture were enriched by his meetings with Hungarian artists. Liszt composed his symphonic poem *Hungaria* (1854) in reply to the ode that poet Mihály Vörösmarty (1800–55) had addressed to him in 1840. That said, quite a few Hungarians turned their backs on him when, in his written work *On the Gypsies and on Gypsy Music in Hungary* (Paris 1859, Budapest 1861) Liszt mistakenly identified what most people called "Gypsy music" with the folk music of the Gypsies themselves; whereas it was in fact composed, ethnic Magyar folk tunes that happened to be interpreted and performed with virtuosity by Gypsies. This caused affront to those non-Gypsy Hungarians none too pleased to see their beloved Magyar music associated with "Gypsy" culture. In Liszt's defense it should be noted that this misimpression about "Gypsy music" lives on to this day among the general public outside of Hungary.

Liszt wrote a portion of his thematically Hungarian works for grand occasions or on commission. For example, he composed *Missa solemnis* (1856) for the consecration of the Esztergom Basilica, and the *Coronation Mass* for the 1867 coronation of Austrian Emperor Francis Joseph as King of Hungary. His other, primarily Hungarian themed oratorio, *The Legend of Saint Elisabeth* (1865), concerned the legendary princess of Hungary's bygone Árpád dynasty, its first and most famous royal line, which endured until 1301. Liszt composed the requiem *Harmonies poétiques et religieuses* with the meaningful subtitle *October 1849* in memory of the thirteen Hungarian generals executed that month by the Austrians in the eastern Hungarian town of Arad (today still Arad, albeit in Romania) and in memory of other reprisals that ensued from Hungary's failed revolution. In his later works, Liszt distilled the more salient Hungarian elements of his earlier, primarily tragic, pathos-filled, and heroic themes to their essence: the *Hungarian Rhapsodies* XVI–XIX and the symphonic poem *From the Cradle to the Grave* (1881–82) as well as the elegy *Sunt lacrimae rerum* from the third of his *Années de Pèlerinage* (Years of Pilgrimage) cycles (1837–77). With his series of piano compositions entitled *Hungarian Historical Portraits*, published in Hungary only in 1956, he erected a musical memorial to his notable Hungarian contemporaries.

To this day, two operas by Liszt's contemporary Ferenc Erkel (1810–93) are performed regularly in Hungary: *Hunyadi László* (1844) and *Bánk bán* (1861). The latter, based on the drama of the same title by József Katona (1791–1830) that expressed the essence of the Hungarian national tragedy, was to become the very paradigm of Hungarian opera. (See the chapter, "Classical Music.") Erkel also set poet Ferenc Kölcsey's *Himnusz* (Anthem) to music, giving Hungary its national anthem.

Hungarian musical history credits the oeuvres of the nation's two foremost modernist composers, Béla Bartók (1881–1945) and Zoltán Kodály (1882–1967), with ending the reign of popular, composed "folk" tunes and bringing to the forefront classical music that drew instead on authentic, previously not composed, bona fide folk music. (See the chapter, "Classical Music.") Indeed, it was this different source of inspiration that goes to explain

Ferenc (Franz) Liszt (1811–86)

why Liszt's thematically Hungarian works are in fact closer to those works that Brahms and Schubert wrote in an ostensibly Hungarian style, than they are to the works of Bartók or Kodály.

Bartók composed his *Dance Suite* (1923) as the musical expression of the ideal of brotherhood between different peoples; and it was likewise in this spirit that he composed *Cantata profana* (1930). However, he did so in an era not particularly amenable to such ideals—after Hungary lost two-thirds of its territory to neighboring states in the 1920 Treaty of Trianon. Although in the eyes of the world Bartók stands as Hungary's foremost twentieth-century composer of international stature, rarely are his thematically Hungarian works performed on the international stage.

By contrast, Kodály, on the basis of his work both as a composer and as a musical educator, is regarded more as a classic "national artist." His works *Székely fonó* (Székely Spinnery, 1932), *Felszállott a páva* (Peacock Variations, 1938–39), and *Háry János* (1926) are based on Hungarian folk songs, and it was the choral oratorio *Psalmus Hungaricus* (1923) that first won him international recognition. In his second group of works—including *Budavári Te Deum* (1936), composed to commemorate the anniversary of Buda's liberation from the Turks—the national style is expressed indirectly.

More recent Hungarian composers were to embark on yet newer roads, as represented for example by the works of György Kurtág (1926). Most prominent among Kurtág's compositions, which constitute a virtuoso response to broad European musical tradition, is *Vonósnégyes* (String Quartet, 1956). Both Kurtág and György Ligeti (1923) left Hungary and made homes abroad. Indeed, Ligeti's works could be heard publicly in his native land for the first time only in 1971, with a performance of *Kamarakoncert* (Chamber Concert). The works of Péter Eötvös (1944)—which, in his own words, extend "the possibilities of composition from strict editing (*Now, Miss!*) to free improvisation (*Music for New York*)"—are performed throughout the world. Eötvös's opera *Three Sisters* (1997) has been staged internationally by leading opera companies with considerable success. In his concerto *Snatches of a Conversation* (2001), classical music meets with lighter fare by way of jazz.

On to the realm of popular music: Hungarian operetta embarked on its international career toward the start of the twentieth century. (See the previous chapter, "Operetta.") However, this was preceded in 1904 by the most popular Hungarian musical stage work ever, *János vitéz* (John the Valiant), by Pongrác Kacsóh (1873–1923). Only the works of the two greats of Hungarian operetta, Imre Kálmán (1882–1953) and Ferenc Lehár (1870–1948), can compete with the popularity of this musical. Lehár's *A víg özvegy* (The Merry Widow, 1905) and *Cigányszerelem* (Gypsy Love, 1910) and Kálmán's *Cigányprímás* (Gypsy Band Leader, 1912), *Csárdáskirálynô* (Csárdás Queen, 1915), and *Marica grófnô* (Countess Marica, 1924) are Hungarian classics of the genre's Viennese variety. Hungarian operettas representing the more dance-rich English variety include *Bob herceg* (Prince Bob, 1903), by Jenő Huszka (1875–1960); and *Leányvásár* (The Marriage Market, 1911), by Viktor Jacobi (1883–1921).

Although operetta's golden age unfolded over the first two decades of the twentieth century, exceptional artists continued to mine this genre, including Szabolcs Fényes (1912–86), who not only wrote the scores for no less than 130 films and composed several hundred hit songs, many of them perennial favorites to this day, but also found the time and inspiration to write more than fifty operettas.

By the 1960s, the Beat movement had the greatest influence on Hungary's popular music scene. (See the chapter, "Light Music.") One musical pair in particular stands out from among the era's rich menu: Levente Szörényi (1945) and János Bródy (1946). They wrote their first songs together, and later they divided the work: Szörényi composed while Bródy did the lyrics. It was a winning recipe. Indeed, they get the credit for the most successful and popular Hungarian light music stage production of recent decades, the rock opera *István, a király* (Stephen the King, 1983).

# music-makers

## Orsolya Nádor

What is often said about Hungarian scientists also goes for Hungary's musical artists: no one is a prophet in his own land. We Hungarians have had no few world-famous singers, instrumental artists, and composers who were known only to a narrow, elite slice of the public at home; whereas abroad, their many admirers perhaps didn't even know they were Hungarian. These days in Hungary we are inclined to include them among our nation's greats no matter where their talent flourished.

Relative to the nation's population, Hungary has given the world a surprising number of musical artists. The reasons for this are hard to pin down, though they lie partly in our nation's unusually strong tradition of musical education, and in part in the enhanced sense of obligation or compulsion (or both) that exceptional artists from small countries often feel to prove themselves before the world.

Hungary's first famous music-maker of bygone days was the lute virtuoso Bálint Bakfark (1507–76), who performed not only in the courts of the Hungarian nobility but crossed the whole of Europe. Many Hungarian musicians, such as János Bihari and János Lavotta, were known and loved in eighteenth- and nineteenth-century Vienna, where they entertained audiences chiefly with *verbunkos* (recruitment style) tunes. Nineteenth-century Europe knew the virtuoso pianist and composer we called Liszt Ferenc as Franz Liszt. (See the chapters, "Composers" and "Classical Music.")

Politics forced many of our musical artists to leave Hungary for extended periods, sometimes for good. And yet other artists were driven from one country to another more so by a desire to hone their professional talents in a way that would have been difficult, if not impossible, at home. Then, once they had learned most everything there was to learn, and once they had made music together with everyone abroad whose music they admired, either they settled somewhere else or returned to Hungary to try their luck back home.

The composer and pianist György Solti (1912–97) was known to the world at large by the name Sir George Solti. First compelled to leave his homeland in 1939, he returned after World War II to resume his work in the Hungarian State Opera. But, as his services were in demand neither as a *répétiteur* nor as a conductor, he left again. Solti lived for years in Germany, and then—by the time he was already widely known and well respected in the musical world—in England. Another celebrated Hungarian pianist, András Schiff, who launched his career simultaneously with a talented bunch of fellow Hungarian pianists including Zoltán Kocsis, Jenő Jandó, and Dezső Ránki, became good friends with Solti. After the master's death, Schiff wrote of Solti's ambivalent relationship with his homeland that although Solti had become famous on account of Béla Bartók, for years he refused to speak Hungarian. He returned to Hungary only after the collapse of the communist regime. Solti gave a concert, supported young artists, and established a foundation. Wrote Schiff, "His love for his mother tongue revived, and he was happy to have the opportunity to speak Hungarian, in particular if he didn't want everyone to understand what he was saying." Although Solti was most at home in the world of opera, his second greatest love became symphonic music, and he achieved world fame as the conductor for the London and Chicago philharmonics.

Virtuosity has characterized a striking share of Hungary's musical artists since the days of Bálint Bakfark. This is true of both singers and instrumental artists; for example, the organist Xavér Varnus, who, born in the mid-1960s, still represents a relatively young generation. Violinist Miklós Szenthelyi, seeking new paths of opportunity for illustrious young talents, founded the Hungarian Virtuosos' Chamber Orchestra in 1988.

The best of our nation's opera singers have spent years as guest artists with the world's greatest operas. Opera lovers both in Hungary and abroad know the names of Éva Marton, Sylvia Sass, Andrea Rost, Erika Miklósa, József Gregor, László Polgár, and other magnificent Magyars. (It might also be noted that most of our opera stars who are old enough and whose repertoires allowed, sung at least once under the direction of György Solti.) In addition to having taken the stage at the Hungarian State Opera, these artists have performed at a whole range of distinguished venues including the Scala in Milan and the Metropolitan in New York, as well as the Vienna, Frankfurt, Munich, and Los Angeles opera houses. What they all have in common is this: before achieving world fame they regularly won prizes or achieved distinction at prestigious singing competitions; and this, in effect, served as entry tickets to the world's great opera houses.

Thankfully, Hungary also has its share of musical artists who have drawn the attention of music-loving audiences *to* Hungary; and, often enough, these artists have managed to do so only by defying the political parties and the governments of the day, not to mention top-ranking officials in charge of cultural policy. For example, two Hungarian orchestras have carved out international renown for themselves in recent decades: the Budapest Festival Orchestra, established in 1983 under the direction of Iván Fischer and Zoltán Kocsis; and the successor of the Hungarian State Concert Orchestra, the National Philharmonic Orchestra, which has been led by Zoltán Kocsis since 1997.

It would be impossible here to introduce all the many ambassadors of Hungarian culture, who, as instrumental or vocal artists, or as conductors, have made names for themselves in the history books of world music. Indeed, newer and newer generations of exceptionally talented musical artists are appearing on the scene all the time; and concert-goers are sure to encounter more than a few of them in the celebrated theaters of both Hungary and the wider world.

# theater

## Adrienn Szentesi

The nineteenth-century saw most peoples of Europe establish their core national institutions, and national theatres were no exception. The history of Hungary's National Theater began in 1832. The most prominent Hungarian politician of the time, Count István Széchenyi, dreamt up a site on the bank of the Danube in Pest. Given that Pest consisted mostly of a German-speaking population in the 1830s, it seemed high time to let the Magyar tongue shine, too, in the institutional form a theater could provide. And that is just what the Hungarian Parliament did in 1836 when it voted to found an "illustrious national theater." The National Theater finally opened in 1840, at the corner of Rákóczi Street and Múzeum Boulevard in Budapest. (A plaque marking this spot can be found today at the Astoria stop of the number 7 bus route.)

The first golden age of this new institution was a long one, stretching from its founding to 1894. Its directors during this era included, among others, Ede Szigligeti (1814–1878) and Ede Paulay (1836–1894). Their talent and enthusiasm did much for the National Theater. In 1913 the theater was razed, and it was given a new space in the home of another theater, the *Népszínház*, on Blaha Lujza Square. To this day this is the place and the building that, to many Hungarians, is synonymous with the very notion of Hungary's *national theater*.

And so the theater enjoyed its second golden age. In 1922 the Minister of Culture, Kunó Klebelsberg, appointed a new director, Sándor Hevesi (1873–1939), who proceeded to complement the theater's stars such as Gizi Bajor and Árpád Ódry with newly hired faces including Árpád Lehotay and Anna Tőkés. Seeking to be known for a more attractive repertoire, the theater strove to commission works by contemporary dramatists. In 1924 it established the National Repertory Theater as a venue for alternative drama. (This initiative established a precedent for similar ventures at many other theaters; indeed, today, most every large theater in Hungary has a repertory theater that hosts pieces allowing for relatively profound theatrical experiences.) Although the National Theater never did depart from European fashions and methods while under Sándor Hevesi's direction, it did carve out for itself a reputation as a one-of-a-kind, truly *national* theater. A great many dramas found their way to its stage during his reign, with new ones debuting almost every two weeks. From 1935 the theater came under the direction of Antal Németh (1903–68), who followed mostly in Hevesi's footsteps. Németh hired the era's greatest performers; for example, Gyula Csortos, Artúr Somlay, and the most popular actor of the day, Pál Jávor.

After World War II the National Theater came under the direction of Tamás Major (1910–86). Eventually, however, the landmark building suffered the same fate as its predecessor: it was razed on April 23, 1965, to make room for a new subway line. Whether tearing it down was necessary is debated to this day. The National Theater company moved temporarily into the former Magyar Theater, which, ironically but also appropriately, happened to be on Sándor Hevesi Square. This provisional headquarters was to last for thirty-four years.

From 1978 the National Theater embarked on one of its most exciting periods. The manager, Péter Nagy, hired Gábor Székely and Gábor Zsámbéki, who were then working in outlying areas of the country, to serve as codirectors. Theirs was a theater developed meticulously to meet the highest standards. It was home to our nation's greatest actors, and to first-rate productions that defined a new era of Hungarian theatrical history.

Meanwhile, the National Theater endeavored to expand its repertoire—which comprised mostly classical, romantic works grounded in a traditional style of delivery—in the direction of modern theater. It therefore forged a dual reputation for itself as both a conservative-cum-traditional venue and an increasingly progressive theater that had a certain flair for the daring and exciting. However, in 1982 its codirectors were transferred from their posts. They went on to establish Budapest's Katona József Theater. Gábor Zsámbéki was still director there as of 2009. The Katona, as it's often called, is one of Hungary's finest venues of theatrical art, with an illustrious company that is ever innovating, ever rejuvenating the definition of Hungarian theater. Back at the National Theater, meanwhile, the end of Zsámbéki and Székely's codirectorial era also brought a close to the reputation for artistic excellence the theater had earned during their reign.

To Hungarians, there are few things more important than their cherished national institutions, and it appears that every era must build its own National Theater. In the mid-1990s it seemed that a decades-long dream was about to be realized: the building of a new national theater began. However, as in days past, the National Theater fell victim to political disputes. After its previously design-ated site in the heart of downtown Budapest was abandoned, a new National Theater (www.nemzetiszinhaz.hu) finally opened in March 2002 just south of downtown, right beside the Danube on the Pest side of the river, between the Petőfi Bridge and the Lágymányosi Bridge. The theater strives to abide by the principles that have always been central to Hungary's National Theater: to present numerous works, contemporary and classical alike. Its repertoire has even been making room once again for alternative approaches. With this, we can only hope that the National Theater's many years of ups and downs have drawn to a close. Will we be saying the same thing thirty or forty years from now?

# film directors

## Adrienn Szentesi

Filmmaking really got underway in Hungary in the 1910s, when silent films became increasingly popular. Two of the most distinguished directorial names illuminating this era are Sándor Korda (1893–1956)—Sir Alexander Korda, as the world later came to know him—and Mihály Kertész (1888–1962). As a producer, Korda set the standard high at the Corvin Film Works, and in doing so he laid the foundations of Hungarian filmmaking. As for Kertész, he applied experience he'd acquired abroad back in Hungary.

After the collapse of the short-lived communist revolution of 1919, both Korda and Kertész opted to try their luck in England. Later they made their way to Hollywood. Among the eventual consequences were the cinema classics *Casablanca* (1942), for which Kertész won an Oscar for best director, and Sándor Korda's *The Thief of Baghdad* (1940), which took home three Oscars.

Subsequent Hungarian directors were also known to forge careers for themselves in Hollywood. During the 1930s, Hungary's own film industry produced a spate of light, romantic comedies. Between 1934 and 1938 nearly 150 films were made in Hungary. After 1938, however, the industry's greatest talents left the country: István Székely, Béla Gaál, and László Vajda. The work they'd done in foreign lands contributed substantially to America's becoming a film industry power to reckon with.

The first Hungarian sound film to achieve lasting artistic value was *Emberek a havason* (People on the Snowy Mountain), which won the 1942 Grand Prix at the Venice Biennial and was directed by István Szőts. With this film, Szőts became a harbinger of Italian neorealism, which heralded the start of a new era in the history of Hungarian film. His innovation rested in a striking realism, the pure naïveté of characters, and the use of outdoor settings.

Hungary's most successful cinematic work of the 1950s was *Körhinta* (Merry-go-round). Directed by Zoltán Fábri (1917–94), this is a beautiful love story that unfolds in a village setting. While the film failed to get the top prize at Cannes in 1956, according to François Truffaut it deserved it. Fábri's films are characterized by a certain disintegrated quality, a singular expressiveness, an emphasis on fantasy, and a fragmentation of time.

Our three greatest living directors as of this writing are Károly Makk (1925), Miklós Jancsó (1921), and István Szabó (1938).

Makk earned an international reputation with his film about instincts and passions, *Ház a sziklák alatt* (House Under the Rocks), which won top prize at the 1958 San Francisco International Film Festival. While his films are characterized by a pronounced aestheticism and a powerful sense of the visual, he was influenced above all by the French *nouvelle vague*. He reached the zenith of his career with *Love* (1970), starring Mari Törőcsik and Iván Darvas as the couple in love.

Miklós Jancsó was also influenced by the French new wave, especially by the films of Michelangelo Antonioni. This helps explain his technical innovations such as long takes. His film *Szegénylegények* (The Hopeless Ones; 1965) marks the start of a new era for Hungarian film. Here, Jancsó created a veritable film ballad. In 1979, Jancsó's life work was recognized in Cannes with a special prize. In *Szörnyek évadja* (Season of Monsters; 1986) he opened a new phase in his oeuvre by applying a new narrative technique, that of video. This film netted him a special prize at the International Venice Film Festival. The recurring protagonists of his most recent films—which include *Nekem lámpát adott kezembe az Úr Pesten* (The Lord's Lantern in Budapest; 1999) and *Kelj fel komám, ne aludjál* (Wake Up, Mate, Don't Sleep!; 2002)—are Kapa and Pepe, an aggressive businessman and a hopeless dupe, stereotypical figures of Hungarian society today. Marked by a laid-back, liberated sense of improvisation, jump-cuts, super–close-ups, and playfulness, these films show that Jancsó is still capable of innovation even at the age of eighty.

For his part, István Szabó has indisputably carved out a place for himself in international film history. In 1981 his film *Mephisto* won an Oscar for Best Foreign Film. Szabó began his career in the spirit of the French New Wave with confessional, lyrical films: *Álmodozások kora* (Age of Reveries), *Apa* (Dad; 1966), and *Szerelmesfilm* (Love Film; 1970). These films concern the various dilemmas afflicting his peers, the search for a path in life, and the emotions that bind people. Szabó's next major filmmaking phase comprises works that speak suggestively about individuals who lose their identity—*Mephisto* (1981), *Redl ezredes* (Colonel Redl; 1984), and *Hanussen* (1988). In these films he returns to classical storytelling. The protagonist in all three works, which comprise a trilogy of sorts, is played by the famed Austrian actor Klaus Maria Brandauer.

Beyond the Oscar for *Mephisto*, Szabó's films have won him numerous other instances of international recognition: two Oscar nominations, a British Academy Film Award, and a special prize at Cannes (for *Colonel Redl*). The protagonists of his 1991 film *Édes Emma, drága Böbe* (Sweet Emma, Dear Böbe), which won a Silver Bear at the Berlin International Film Festival, struggle to get by amid Hungary's new, post–communist era social realities.

Since the late 1990s Szabó has directed several films as international coproductions. With Ralph Fiennes in the lead, *Sunshine* (1999)—released in Hungary under the title *A Napfény íze* (The Taste of Sunshine)—is the story of three generations in the life of a single Jewish family. This film earned a European Film Award and an American National Society of Film Critics Award. Szabó's 2001 film *Taking Sides*—released in Hungary as *Szembesítés* (Confrontation)—starring Harvey Keitel, concerns the life of the famous German composer Wilhelm Furtwängler. *Being Julia* (2004)—released in Hungary under the title *Csodálatos Júlia*

(Wonderful Julia)—starred Jeremy Irons and Anette Bening, and won Bening a Golden Globe award for best actress. With *Rokonok* (Relatives; 2006), about small-town corruption, Szabó returned to film production in his native land after many years of doing so abroad.

This account cannot close without mention of the newest generation of Hungarian filmmakers, who have brought not only new momentum and new perspectives into the world of Hungarian film, but of course also numerous international honors.

What with its singular atmosphere, György Pálfi's *Hukkle* (Hiccup; 2002) won the European Film Academy's Fassbinder Prize in 2002 for best first film. His second major film, *Taxidermia* (Taxidermy; 2006), the story of a grandfather, father, and son marked by its singular depiction of the body, of human beauty, won numerous awards and ran in cinemas across Europe. Whatever Kornél Mundruczó does, it earns him recognition and honors. His second film, *Szép napok* (Pleasant Days) won prizes in Brussels and Locarno, and several of his short films subsequently won honors at numerous film festivals outside of Hungary. *Delta* (2008), about the battle between man and nature, earned its place in competition at the Cannes Film Festival. And then there is Benedek Fliegauf, who creates a one-of-a-kind ambience with his mostly black and white, philosophical works. His 2003 film *Rengeteg* (Forest) received the Berlin International Film Festival's Wolfgang Staudte Prize. His 2004 film Dealer won the FIPRESCI prize for best director, and was also honored at the Berlin International Film Festival.

Nimród Antal's *Kontroll* (Control) was a big success, reaping awards at numerous film festivals—including the Youth Prize at Cannes in 2004. This film saw unprecedented popularity in Hungary, despite the fact that its director was previously unknown and that both what it had to say and the mood it created in saying this differed markedly from that of traditional Hungarian films. One thing is certain, though: the film's protagonists, the ticket checkers whose presence so typifies the Budapest metro system, have turned out to be compelling characters for both Hungarian and non-Hungarian audiences alike.

# movie stars

## Adrienn Szentesi

An actor lives a public life, or so it seems to the public. Stars in particular are idols, exemplars. They are the faces, the characters, nay, the archetypes of a nation. Audiences either see in them their own reflections, or else imagine stars' lives to be a realm of the imagination far from their own worlds.

People just love to be in love with their dreams, which helps explain why they love seeing loving couples on the silver screen. The first such classic couple in Hungarian film comprised Katalin Karády (1912–90) and Pál Jávor (1902–59). The fiendish woman and the fiery man. Karády sparked scandal with her unabashed sexuality, her entic-ing droning voice, her exotic femininity. Virtually overnight she became a star, a legend. As for Pál Jávor, who already had an impressive line-up of credits on silent film when the era of sound motion pictures ensued, he acted in nearly fifty films. Both on and off screen he lived a turbulent, carousing life. He embodied the era's ideal Hungarian man: the gentleman, the cavalier, the macho man. Unforgettable scenes were born of Karády and Jávor's encounter in Lajos Zilahy's 1939 film *Halálos tavasz* (Deadly Spring). In this film, Karády broke through the barriers of prudish hypocrisy and stifled sexuality in a single bound. In her famous disrobing scene she revealed things never before seen on screen in Hungary. This legendary couples' other classic film was likewise a Zilahy work, *Valamit visz a víz* (The River is Carrying Something Along). Here too, Karády is a secretive femme fatale, while Jávor writhes away in the woman's net, damned to indecision.

The amorous couple in Zoltán Fábri's *Körhinta* (Merry-go-Round; 1955), played by Mari Törőcsik (1935) and Imre Soós (1930–57), drew tears from the eyes of every viewer. Indeed, the film's famous merry-go-round scene—in which the man calls out to his love, "We're flying, Mari!"—has become an iconic picture in Hungary. Törőcsik was received in Cannes as a bona fide star after the film's screening. Although her performance in this film deserved it, twenty years later she finally did win the best actress award in Cannes for her role in the film *Déryné* (Mrs. Déry). She performed in almost sixty films, playing her characters with a staggering insight that yielded a natural effect. She is truly a born talent, with a profound sense of style. Her leading man, Imre Soós, died with tragic suddenness at a young age, but in the approximately one dozen films he made in the space of his short career, his legendary figure, his searing eyes, his inner fire, and his mischievous smile were immortalized on the silver screen.

Zoltán Latinovits (1931–76) succeeded Imre Soós as the archetypal Hungarian male lead. The Magyar man. We could see Latinovits in more than fifty films and countless stage roles. His sonorous voice gave new life to the classics of Hungarian poetry. He played his first defining screen role in Miklós Jancsó's *Oldás és kötés* (English title: *Cantata*; 1963) with Edit Domján in the female lead. He gave an unforgettable performance in Zoltán Huszárik's 1971 film *Szindbád*, an adaptation of a  series of Gyula Krúdy's classic early twentieth-century stories about the inveterate romantic of this name. In this role, Latinovits became the seducer, the eccentric, the love of married women and lovely maidens; the wistful, fog-enveloped knight. With impeccable insight he delivered the role of this perpetual daydreamer who inhabits a magical world. No one can spread marrow on toast and then bring it to his mouth with such feeling as can Latinovits in *Szindbád*. No one can wait for a woman as Latinovits waited as Szindbád. His remarkable voice is with us to this day; it rings in our ears, and, indeed, it titillated every Hungarian woman who ever heard it. Latinovits costarred in this film with Éva Ruttkai (1927–86), the starry-eyed actress he did in fact live with. Indeed, they comprised the most celebrated "husband-and-wife" acting team in Hungarian theatrical history.

Of course, Hungary's silver screen has played host to other lovebirds as well. Never will we forget Iván Darvas and Mari Törőcsik in Károly Makk's film *Szerelem* (Love; 1971). Or the celebrated 1980s actress Ildikó Bánsági and actor Péter Andorai in István Szabó's *Bizalom* (Confidence; 1980). Judit Pogány and Róbert Koltai in *Szívzűr* (Heartache; 1982) and *Panelkapcsolat* (Prefab People; 1982). What two names will go down in the annals of Hungarian cinematic history as the great romantic couple of the first decades of the twenty-first century? Who will we find to envy on the silver screen? We do not know. Or do we? We can, after all, already sit back and wonder at the loving couple played by Gabriella Hámori and Sándor Csányi in Incze Ágnes's *I Love Budapest* (2001) and Péter Bergendy's *Állítsátok meg Terézanyut!* (Stop Mom Theresa!; 2004).

# photographers

## Noémi Kiss

We can't help but turn a bit sentimental if the subject turns to our nation's photographic heritage. After all, the golden age of Hungarian photography ended long ago, having developed (no pun intended) sometime around the turn of the twentieth century and come to a crashing end with the collapse of the Austro-Hungarian Monarchy in 1918. Indeed, the history of Hungarian photography is itself like an old camera—it is a history fixed in the images of a vanished past. Perhaps this is why, when looking upon the pictures of Hungarian photographers of that era, we see almost nothing but melancholic and nostalgia-permeated faces: the woeful expressions of the poets Endre Ady and Mihály Babits; those of men with their money-making dancing monkeys at outdoor markets; the solitary beauty of a bleak agricultural landscape, perhaps punctuated by the tower of a wooden church in Transylvania; or else a bare-breasted Gypsy girl.

The masters of early Hungarian photography quickly became world famous. However, politics forced some to leave their homelands. Thus, the world came to know the so-called "Hungarian style" of photography through the work of André Kertész and Robert Capa. That's not to mention Brassaï (pseudonym of Gyula Halász), who rose to fame in Paris (where Kertész tutored him); and Martin Munkácsi, who (like Kertész and Capa) made his way via Europe to the United States, and one of whose early works inspired the great photographer Henri Cartier-Bresson to remark, "For me this photograph was the spark that ignited my enthusiasm. I suddenly realized that, by capturing the moment, photography was able to achieve eternity."

The Hungarian style actually comprises two traditions. One of these is urban or city photography, which György Klösz (1844–1913) lifted to a high standard from 1873 on with his photographs of a newly united Buda and Pest. He drew on the so-called wet colloidal process, which revolutionized photographic technique. Around the same time, photographer Károly Divald was experimenting with similar techniques in his studio in the northern town of Eperjes (today Prešov, Slovakia).

Meanwhile, "peasant" or rural photography emerged at the very same time with the documentary images of Mór Erdélyi and Rudolf Balogh, who photographed Transylvanian landscapes, farms, and notable historic events. This tradition was the predecessor of the "ethnographic" photography of today.

Yet another factor also drove the fast-paced changes in Hungarian photography in the second half of the nineteenth century: the arrival of exceptional practitioners from Vienna, Darmstadt, Paris, and London. Some of these photographers only organized exhibits and shows or distributed the latest products of the Kodak company, while others established permanent studios. Three cities above all—Budapest, Kolozsvár (today Cluj-Napoca, Romania), and Eperjes (today Prešov, Slovakia)—became the nation's centers of photography. Hungarian aristocrats established photographic clubs where they reported on their journeys to Transylvania or else much further afield, whether the Middle East or Africa.

In 1882, Ferenc Veress founded the first Hungarian photography magazine, *Fényképészeti lapok* (Photographic Pages). Hungary, with its advanced cultural scene on the photographic front, was a European leader in opening this new window on the world. The aim was to study and amass knowledge of both Hungary's own, national landscape and distant, foreign lands.

As generally was the case across the Monarchy, the expansion of the bourgeoisie and the attendant diffusion of its customs played a big role in the lightning-fast spread of photography in Hungary. By the turn of the century, practically every well-established family, from the bourgeoisie and the peasantry alike, had its own portrait photographer.

The photographer could glimpse into all aspects of life, nay, even into life after death, as it were. Today's traveler who visits cemeteries in the onetime eastern provinces of the Monarchy can be witness to a unique phenomenon—namely, he or she will discover pictures on tombstones, pictures that bring to life the faces of the dead.

Moreover, photography crossed paths with other branches of the arts—above all, literature. One of Hungary's most famous daguerreotypes is of Sándor Petőfi (1823–49), Hungary's freedom-fighting poet. This picture can be seen today at the Petőfi Literary Museum in Budapest. Péter Nádas (1942) is not only among contemporary Hungary's greatest novelists but also a distinguished photographer. His photographic essay *Saját halál* (Own Death), recounts the moving story of his heart attack through 160 pictures of a pear tree in his yard. Meanwhile, antique Hungarian photography can be found in museums as well, from the temporary exhibits at the Mai Manó photo gallery in Budapest (www.maimano.hu) to the Hungarian Museum of Photography in Kecskemét, central Hungary (www.fotomuzeum.hu).

Finally, a question: *who* is the photographer? Who stands behind the camera? In the beginning of the photographic era, the main thing at stake was the technical hurdle of capturing an image of the world; the photographer often remained anonymous. However, it wasn't long before Hungary's print media discovered the power of the photographer. The weekly paper *Vasárnapi Újság* (Sunday News) began publishing pictures in 1870. Later, photography's manipulative potential was felt in Hungary, too. The doctoring of reality through photographs became a virtual science during World War II and, not least, over the ensuing decades of one-party rule. Photographs were used to deceive the public; they served to reinforce the power of dictatorship. For example, in the 1950s party secretary and dictator Mátyás Rákosi, though he was short, was once photographed in such a way as to virtually rise right out of a field of wheat.

Today, in the age of digital photography, everything is changing. As in so many other reaches of the globe, in Hungary practically everyone goes about with a camera and cell phone in hand; indeed, often the

two are built into the same device. Per capita sales of mobile phones and digital cameras in Hungary are among the world's highest. And so it is not much of a stretch to say that, these days, *every* Hungarian is a photographer.

# inventor

## Gábor Vaderna

Does the inventor think away at length, or does a stroke of brilliance pop into his mind in a flash? Does the inventor tinker away in a workshop or ponder away in an armchair? Does he consciously develop an invention, or does this invention come to him at night, in a dream? Does the inventor think fast, or slow? Is his mind all over the place or, quite to the contrary, focused to the hilt? Does the inventor prefer logic-laden crime novels or dreamy romances? For that matter, does the inventor like playing chess? Such questions are hard to answer. One thing is certain, though: a good invention is a simple one.

Take Rubik's Cube—which in Hungary also goes by the names *Bûvös Kocka* (Magic Cube), *Rubik-kocka* (Rubik Cube), and *Magyar Kocka* (Hungarian Cube). Rather simple in structure, the legendary cube has six sides with as many different colors, and with each side divided into nine smaller squares. The center square in each side is in a fixed position, whereas the rest of the squares can be turned around three axes; and so the eight squares whose three sides differ, and the twelve squares whose two sides differ, can change positions. The task is quite simple: the mixed-up squares must be restored to their original positions, so that those of the same color end up on the same side.

No problem! Give me that cube! I turn it left, I turn it right, and still it doesn't work. Hours go by, and finally I'm almost there. Yes, but one of the squares isn't where it should be. Only after several more hours do I realize that I was in fact furthest from the solution when I thought I was closest. I can't stop thinking about it. The next day I again take hold of the cube, and my hand goes about turning it from memory; indeed, the individual combinations seem familiar. And, hey! It worked! But how did I do it? In an instant I mix up the squares again and start all over.

Not even the cube's inventor, Ernő Rubik, suspected that this structure he patented in 1975 would soon become a favorite game all over the world. In 1980 Rubik's Cube was named Toy of the Year in England, and in 1981 it became part of the Architecture and Design collection at New York's Museum of Modern Art. Rubik's Cube fan clubs formed across the globe, and the cube even became the basis of a specialized "cubic cosmology." In 1982, with the participation of the national champions of nineteen countries, Budapest hosted the Rubik's Cube World Championship, which the American Minh Thai won in 22.95 seconds. The *Oxford English Dictionary* officially recognized Rubik's Cube as an English-language term. According to an American physicist, the cube can serve as a model for the structure of a quark. A woman in Düsseldorf filed for divorce because her husband was more in love with Rubik's

Cube than with her. In America, an organization called Cubaholics Anonymous was established to help cube addicts. In 1992 British Prime Minister John Major used the cube to explain the virtually unsolvable complexity of the Maastricht Treaty (whose approval institutionalized today's European Union and led to the euro). And, indeed, some people have recognized in the cube a likeness of the real world—for only in the rarest of instances can order arise from its general state of disorder.

The cube itself is simple and small, but it harbors a virtually infinite number of possibilities. Turning the squares can yield 43,252,003,274,489,856,000 different patterns. This means that if we devote one second to each turn, it will take a mere 1.4 billion years to give every single pattern its one second of fame.

Why was it the Rubik's Cube, of all things, that revolutionized the world's toy industry? Because Ernő Rubik paid heed to details. The cube can be moved in various directions, and yet its pieces don't come apart. The designer paid special attention to the color: the cube's standard color pattern (i.e., when solved!) is such that *yellow* marks the color difference between any two opposite faces of the cube. In other words, white is opposite yellow, red is opposite orange, and blue is opposite green.

The cube's inventor had an ideal mentor from whom to learn meticulous planning. Ernő Rubik's father—likewise an inventor—designed airplanes. Ernő also had one heck of a good place to study: the Budapest Technical University's Department of Architecture. From there he went on to earn a degree from the College of Applied Arts, where he then taught. Ernő Rubik regularly shared his ideas with his students, and so they were the first to try the cube.

So then, what characterizes a good inventor? Above all, an inventor is happy. "The important thing is that my occupation gives me pleasure," Rubik himself once said. As for the author of this article, do excuse me while I have another go at solving the cube.

# philosopher

## Szabolcs Parragh

In terms of both fame and influence, György Lukács (1885–1971)—
better known to the world as Georg Lukacs—was Hungary's most
important philosopher. More precisely, he was a philosopher born
to a Jewish bourgeois family; he wrote in German; and he lived most
of his life, though not all of it, in Hungary. As contradictory as his
career was in key respects, it is nonetheless representative of the era's
intellectual life and times in Hungary. Lukács was on the one hand an
intellectual in the classic sense of the word, one who contributed lasting
accomplishments to philosophy. Even at those times when politics
barred him from public life, he invariably resumed his research and
focused again on his works. And yet Lukács also nurtured political
ambitions; he was a thinker who believed in the value of practical
experience and knowledge, and who, over the course of his life, was
often compelled to humble himself, to retract views he'd professed.
Let us now examine a few moments of his fascinating career:

In the spirit of a true second-generation bourgeois-born rebel—
one who questions the social order in which he was raised—
Lukács, the son of a successful banker, sharply criticized the social
circumstances that made his father's success and that of others like
him possible. He did so even in his early, aesthetics-oriented works;
works that, unlike his later writings, were still grounded in German
idealism. Lukács would later call his youthful thinking "romantic
anticapitalism," though it must be said that he gave up only the
romantic aspect of this attribute when he turned toward Marxism.

Bourgeois or not, his background as such made it possible for
Lukács to join up with European intellectual life—and in the Hungary

of that era, "European," in this sense, at least, meant *German*. In his twenties he moved to Heidelberg, where he established professional ties with the Marxist philosopher Ernst Bloch, the sociologist Georg Simmel, as well as the sociologist Max Weber and his circle. In his great novel *The Magic Mountain*, Thomas Mann modelled the character of Naphta, who advocated terror and was given to long intellectual debates, on Lukács's thinking.

Later, Lukács traveled home regularly to Hungary, where he became an important member of the leftist intellectual elite. His radicalism spurred him to action, and so in 1918 he joined the Communist Workers Party of Hungary (KMP). After the 1919 communist takeover, during the reign of the short-lived Council Republic, Lukács joined the government as commissar of education. With the overthrow of this regime after a few months, however, he fled Hungary. Lukács was able to return home only in 1945, once Soviet forces had occupied his native land. He then received a university professorship, became a member of parliament, and was elected to the Academy of Sciences.

With the onset of one-party rule in 1948, Lukács became a key figure among those Hungarian intellectuals who lent their ideological support to the communist dictatorship. During the 1956 revolution he again assumed the role of reformer, when he accepted the position of Minister for Peoples' Education. In consequence, with the revolution's defeat he was again forced out of public life in Hungary; this time, for nearly ten years.

Between the world wars Lukács passed his exile first in Vienna and then, from 1929, in the Soviet Union, although he traveled often to Germany. He was an influential member of the international communist organization Comintern. Since his views and the movement's interests often clashed, however, Lukács was compelled to learn the theatrical gesture of public apology. In 1929 he openly denounced the Blum theses he had submitted to the KMP only a year earlier. In those writings, which concerned the orientation the party would adopt if it came to power in Hungary, he had recommended a platform contrary to the orthodoxy of the Marxist-Leninist model.

Years later, in the course of Hungary's *Lukács-vita* (Lukács debate), which erupted in 1949, some declared several of Lukács's doctrines to be infused with "rightist deviation." This led Lukács to another round of public self-criticism. After being accused of neglecting Soviet and socialist-realist literature, he saw to the publication of an anthology of works by Soviet writers. Hungary's standard encyclopedia in the communist era from 1961 onward, the *Új Magyar lexikon* (New Hungarian Encyclopedia), commented as follows on Lukács: "[H] is revisionist views have been analyzed thoroughly since 1957 by Marxist criticism."

Published in 1923, Lukács's *Geschichte und Klassenbewusstsein* (History and Class Consciousness) is one of the defining works of twentieth-century Marxist philosophy. For decades it served as a special point of reference for Marxist thinkers. According to sociologist Lucien Goldman, Martin Heidegger conceived his *Being and Time* (1927) partly in response to Lukács's views. As a teacher, Lukács founded a veritable school of philosophy in Hungary. His students, members of the so-called Budapest School—including Ágnes Heller, Mihály Vajda, Miklós Almási, Ferenc Fehér, and others—have gone on to become defining figures of intellectual life both in Hungary and, in some cases, abroad.

Cover of German edition of one of Lukacs's early works, *Soul and Form*

György (Georg) Lukacs (1885–1971)

# scientists

## Gábor Vaderna

Four Hungarian physicists are playing poker in the United States of America in the early 1950s. All four were raised in Budapest in the first decades of the twentieth century, all four studied to be engineers, all four earned their doctoral degrees in Germany, and all four—owing to their Jewish descent—wound up in America. Without these four men, modern life would not be what it is.

The youngest, Edward Teller (1908–2003)—this man Hungarians know by his original, Magyar name, *Teller Ede*—stares long and hard at his cards; he prefers ping-pong. The oldest, Leo Szilárd (1898–1964), thinks Teller is bluffing. Eugene Wigner (1902–95)—who is no *Eugene*, to Hungarians, but *Jenő*—smiles unassumingly; he calls it quits in the next round. But everyone is waiting for the fourth one of them, John von Neumann (1903–57). ("John? *von?*" A Hungarian might say. "Surely you mean *Neumann János!*") Neumann thinks a long time; he doesn't play by intuition but instead mentally processes all possible card combinations. Today we would say that his mind works "like a computer."

While Neumann is busy counting, let us see just who these men around this table are. Leo Szilárd is the father of countless patents. His idea for the neutron chain reaction (1934), which came to him while walking on a London street, theoretically opened the door to the making of an atomic weapon. Later he and Albert Einstein wrote a letter to Franklin Delano Roosevelt calling the President's attention to the importance of developing such a weapon. After Germany's surrender, he tried desperately to halt its use. Indeed, Szilárd dedicated his life to ensuring that this atomic energy he himself had been so instrumental in removing from its Pandora's Box should not mean an end to human civilization. Szilárd appealed to both Kennedy and Khrushchev, and he repeatedly worked out plans to convince the two Cold War adversaries to dismantle their nuclear arsenals. He even published a utopian-satirical short-story collection on the subject, *The Voice of Dolphins*.

Szilárd showed that atomic energy could be used for purposes other than weaponry. Together with Enrico Fermi he patented the inhomogeneous atomic reactor using a three-dimensional lattice of uranium slugs dropped into holes in blocks of graphite, with sliding neutron-absorbing cadmium control rods to regulate the chain reaction—which is to say, they discovered the atomic power plant.

These Hungarian scientists playing cards around this table didn't see eye to eye on everything with Szilárd the peacenik. While Wigner and Neumann also opposed the use of the atomic bomb, they didn't stand in the way of arsenal-building, whereas for his part, Edward Teller actually helped further the whole process.

Teller, too, had worked in Los Alamos during World War II, and later he became the lead scientist for America's atomic weapons development program. As he saw it, world peace could be guaranteed only if both sides had a weapons arsenal of the same size; for as soon as one side would achieve superiority, it would use its weapons. This was the logic that led Teller to work out the theory of thermonuclear reactions: the idea that opposing light atomic nuclei could easily achieve fusion at high temperatures, releasing great energy. That is, he discovered the hydrogen bomb.

Eugene Wigner, meanwhile, was the greatest Hungarian scientist of all time. As a young man, he applied the symmetries of nature to develop the foundations of quantum mechanics, for which he received the Nobel Prize in 1963. During World War II he designed so-called Hanford reactors, which produced plutonium for the atomic bombs. He designed and built the first high-output, water-cooled reactors, and he was the world's first nuclear reactor engineer. Eighteen universities gave him honorary doctorates. All the same, this world famous scientist held John von Neumann to be the world's smartest man.

Just who is this von Neumann still racking his brains over his next move in the poker game? His was the genius that developed the mathematically sound axiomatic foundation of quantum mechanics—mathematical game theory—and who designed and built computers that not only stored data but that could also be programmed to perform operations. Without the first of these, modern physics would not exist; without the second, there would be no modern mathematics; and without the third, there would be no computer age. Von Neumann was invited everywhere to count: Tódor Kármán, who was likewise born and raised in Hungary, sought out his help in designing the supersonic airplane; and at Los Alamos, von Neumann was called upon to simulate nonlinear shock waves. This is not to mention his calculation of the mutual effect of various weather patterns and his prediction of the greenhouse effect. When von Neumann recognized the limits of his own thinking—not even he could calculate everything, after all!—he developed, almost as an aside, the foundations of modern computing. United States presidents and generals asked him for strategic advice, and as a member of the U.S. Atomic Energy Commission he had considerable say over the fate of the world.

Four great minds. And this was but the tip of the iceberg: we haven't yet said a thing about their lesser discoveries and inventions, and not a thing about these scientists' students. Nor do we know why *them* in particular. What could their secret have been? Wigner once remarked that after secondary school physics, he didn't hear much new in college. According to Szilárd, the best thing about studying physics on the university level in Hungary was that the classes were so lousy that the students had to figure out everything for themselves.

Was it the good secondary school? The poor university? Or did Budapest's cultural life help these four scientists blossom? In all probability it was the fortunate and unfortunate confluence of several factors: historical traumas, the persecution of Jews as fascism gathered force, the lure of America. What's certain is that these four men were not the only Magyar minds whose lives took similar paths. Indeed, there were so many Hungarian scientists in 1950s America that a rumor spread: these brilliant minds who speak English with a singular accent and communicate with each other in an alien tongue probably arrived straight from Mars. Blind luck or fate? We cannot know.

In the meantime, we've missed the end of the card game. Ultimately, Neumann went down in defeat. He may have penned an article on the mathematics of poker, but fate saw to it that not even he could get a handle on luck.

# travelers & explorers

## István Bori

"To sea, Hungarians!" declared Lajos Kossuth in the mid-nineteenth century, suggesting in no uncertain terms that Hungarians must carve out their place in maritime shipping and commerce. Neither then nor since then has this objective been realized, of course, for with neither a sea nor ports, we Hungarians didn't have much of a chance. Hungarians remained what they were (and *where* they were): travelers and explorers of dry land.

More specifically: travelers from aristocratic families, linguists who practically devote their lives to scholarship, or adventurers in love with the achievements of new technology. Even if the world's most celebrated travelers and explorers aren't Hungarian, there were—as we shall now see—a few whose names have not been forgotten.

These days perhaps the world's most well-known Hungarian traveler-explorer is László Almásy (1895–1951), whose life was the subject of the novel *The English Patient*, which in movie form received no less than nine Oscars in 1996. A fiercely competitive sportsman and a champion of modern technology, Almásy tested a passenger car in Egypt by driving it across several thousand miles of desert, and in Cairo he established a flying school. The foremost scientific achievement of his life of adventures and adventurous twists was his mapping of the unknown heart of the Sahara. What is more, along the banks of the Nile at the border of Sudan and Egypt, he happened upon the so-called Magyarabs—a people who, according to their tradition, were the descendants of Magyars who had wound up in Africa hundreds of years earlier, and who had proudly gone by this name ever since.

László Almásy wasn't yet born when Count Sámuel Teleki (1845–1916) embarked on an African expedition in 1886. Along with Ludwig von Höhnel, who drew up exceptional maps during their travels, Teleki headed out from the island of Zanzibar to explore East Africa, which was virtually unknown to outsiders at the time. In the course of their journey—which was not without its dangers, for they often skirmished with natives who were fighting colonialists—they discovered a lake they named Lake Rudolf after the successor to the Austrian crown (today Lake Turkana) and a 646-meter high volcano south of the lake. This volcano today bears Teleki's name, as does a valley, a lake, and a rest-house in the vicinity of Mount Kenya, not

Count Sámuel Teleki (1845–1916)

to mention a lovely flower that grows to more than three-feet high, *Lobelia Teleki*. In the course of their expedition they also discovered another important lake, a salt lake they named after Stefania, Rudolf's wife.

In terms of scientific-scholarly achievement, Hungary's most prominent traveler was perhaps Sándor Kőrösi Csoma (1784–1842), who lives on in the pages of history books abroad as Alexander Csoma de Koros. As a little boy born to a poor Transylvanian family, his dream was to travel east and discover the ancient Hungarian homeland. On completion of his studies in Transylvania and in Germany, Kőrösi Csoma left for Asia in 1819. On arriving in the Himalayas he began, with British government sponsorship, to study the Tibetan language. In a hidden little corner of the then-independent kingdom of Ladakh, he learned the Tibetan language and immersed himself in the mysteries of Buddhism with the help of lamas while staying in their monastery. With this new knowledge,

Kőrösi Csoma wrote his two major works, both of which were published in Calcutta in 1834. His *Tibetan-English Dictionary* and *Tibetan Grammar* earned Kőrösi Csoma an enduring reputation as a founder of Tibetology. In an odd twist of fate, however, he never did have the chance to realize his original aim of finding the ancestral Hungarian homeland, for he died in the course of his long journey. The tombstone of Sándor Kőrösi Csoma (which presumably reads, "Alexander Csoma de Koros"), who learned seventeen languages both living and dead in his lifetime, is to be found in Darjeeling, India.

Sándor Kőrösi Csoma (1784–1842)

Hungary can lay claim to at least one significant achievement as recently as the late-twentieth century that merits mention here. Following in the footsteps of their great predecessors and taking Kossuth's advice to heart, in 1985 Nándor Fa and József Gál built a yacht, set to sea, and in two years they sailed round the world. Their vessel, the Szent Jupát, is on display at the Budapest Transportation Museum, whose visitors are dumbfounded to this day: "On the oceans in this wee little vessel?! No thanks!"

# world of legends

## Jolán Mann

In the age of Romanticism, when the Hungarian nation was busy focusing on its folk traditions, the great writer János Arany (1817–82) defined the difference between the *népmese* (folk tale) and *népmonda* (folk legend) thus: "The former is a people's epos; the latter, its history." While the legend also depicts miraculous events, like the folk tale, it approaches them differently. A character in a legend experiences a miraculous event as exceptional with respect to reality, while in the world of the folk tale the line between reality and miracle is blurry indeed. Hungarian legends typically belong to one of three categories: origin legends, historical legends, and belief legends.

Hungary's totemic origin legend is the *Legend of the White Stag*, which builds upon an idea that enjoyed considerable currency among Byzantine and Western European historians of the tenth century—namely, that the Magyars were related to the Huns. According to this legend, Hunor and Magor, the forefathers of the Huns and the Magyars, and (in this legend) the two sons of the ardent hunter, Ménrót, are led by a white stag they are chasing to a new homeland, Meotisz, which is rich in fish and game and is on the northern shore of the Black Sea. Settling in this ancient region called Scythia, Hunor occupies the western part; Magor, the eastern part. They secure wives by kidnapping the daughters of the prince of the neighboring Alan people; their warriors, meanwhile, display similar resourcefulness in the context of the times by making off with the daughters' female friends.

The prominence of the white stag in this legend serves to explain

THE ESSENTIAL GUIDE TO BEING HUNGARIAN

why that motif central to the worldview of the pagan Magyars—the tree of life, which, from its roots to its trunk on upward to its crown and beyond, symbolizes the three realms of existence, of the world—has branches that resemble a stag's antlers. While this sort of "world tree" can also be found in the realm of Indo-European beliefs, only in Hungarian folklore do the branches have such a pattern, and only there is the tree topped off by celestial bodies.

Related to Hun legends is the origin legend of a subgroup of Hungarians, the Székelys. As this legend has it, after the death of Attila, the prince of the Huns, his only surviving son and his youngest, the crown prince Csaba, wished to unite with the Magyars to reoccupy Attila's inheritance. Heading off for Scythia (an ancient region centered around the northern coast of the Black Sea), he left behind half the peoples of the Carpathians, the Székelys, but turned back three times to help them in their battles. On the fourth occasion, Csaba, now no longer alive but still bent on saving the Székelys, arrived in Transylvania right out of the sky along the *Hadak útja* (literally: *Triumphal Way*)—that is, the Milky Way.

The notion of a Hun-Magyar relationship is also very much present in those Magyar legends that concern the Huns. For example, in the legend recounting the separation of the Huns and the Magyars there appears that mythical falcon known to Hungarians as the *turulmadár* (literally: turul bird)—the totem animal of the conquering Huns. The *turul* first led the Huns toward the Carpathian Basin, and later provided the same service for their rightful heirs, the Magyars. The *turul-monda* (Turul Legend)—known also as *Álmos-monda* (Legend of Álmos) and *Emese álma* (Emese's Dream)—was the totemic origin legend of the people whom the Magyar chieftan Árpád led into the Carpathian Basin. According to this legend, a turul appeared to Emese, the ancient mother of the Magyars, in her dreams, and it predicted that she would bear a royal dynasty; indeed, another version of this legend has her impregnated by none other than the amorous turul. Her son, Álmos—the father of Árpád—received his name on account of this legendary dream. (*Álmos* in modern-day Hungarian means "sleepy," but in days past it meant also "seen in a dream.")

Hungary's historical legends thus reach back all the way to the time of the Magyar conquest of the Carpathian Basin. Even before arriving in what was to become their new homeland, the seven Magyar tribes tied an alliance that their seven chieftans sealed with their blood. This was the so-called *vérszerzôdés* (blood pact). They chose Álmos as their leader. However, it was his son Árpád who was to lead the Magyars across *Vereckei-szoros* (Verecke Pass) into the Carpathian Basin. Yet another legend, the *fehérló-monda* (Legend of the White Horse), recounts the Magyar conquest of the Carpathian Basin thus: the Magyars acquire the right of settlement and possession from the Moravian leader Svatopluk in exchange for an ornamentally harnessed white horse. In exchange for the horse, they asked "only" for a handful of land, some grass, and a canteen of water, which to them, a nomadic equestrian people, symbolized an entire nation. This incredibly strong horse makes its appearance in Magyar folk tales, too, such as *A fehérlófia* (Son of the White Horse) and *Tündér Ilona* (Ilona the Fairy). And the white horse was also the sacrificial animal of the pagan Magyars.

The two legends associated with the era of the Magyar incursions into various reaches of Europe are the *Lél-monda* (short for Lehel) and *Botond-monda*. At the center of the latter is a plucky Magyar warrior who smashes in Constantinople's golden gate with his mace, easily defeating his giant Greek foe. The *Lél* legend, by contrast, marks the final phase of the Magyar incursions; for it concerns a Magyar chieftain by the name of Lél taken captive in the Battle of Augsburg (955), which the Magyars lost. According to this legend, before his execution he beats the German emperor to death with his horn; which is why the legend is aptly named *Lehel kürtje* (Lehel's Horn).

Prominent among Hungarian historical legends are those concerning heroic leaders, especially King Mátyás (Matthias). The dispenser of justice and redeemer associated with this Hungarian king is an archetypal character also found, with different motifs, in the folklore of neighboring peoples. The recurring motif of Hungarian Matthias legends is that of a king who hides himself among the common folk by going about in disguise—thus acquiring experiences that allow him to make fair decisions for the good of his subjects. The Rákóczi legends and the Kossuth legends, meanwhile, concern the figures of two of Hungary's great freedom fighters of centuries past, Ferenc Rákóczi (1676–1735) and Lajos Kossuth (1802–94).

Hungarian belief legends, which comprise the third major category, typically feature supernatural beings. For example, there is the newborn shaman who possesses miraculous strength, eleven fingers, and teeth (qualities few human babies can lay claim to); and the *garabonciás*, a wizard disguised as a wise, traveling student who is able to literally, demonically raise up a storm—that is, he is capable of both destroying and healing. The shamanic figure of superhuman strength that appears in the folklore of neighboring peoples differs from the Magyar variety—which reaches back to the shamans of the ancient, pagan Magyars—only by acquiring knowledge not through will but through prolonged sleep. While Hungarian legends concerning the origins of the Magyars were preserved in Latin chronicles from the thirteenth and fourteenth centuries, more recent Hungarian legends are known to us today primarily in consequence of active folklore-collecting endeavors of the past two centuries.

Nineteenth-century Hungarian literature sought to reinforce national unity by turning the Magyars' historical and origin legends into epic written works. Nonetheless, genuine popularity went not to the literary epics of Mihály Csokonai Vitéz (1773–1805), Mihály Vörösmarty (1800–55), or János Arany (1817–82), but instead to nineteenth-century Hungary's two great narrative poems, which exemplify the contrasts between those two similar genres, the folk tale and the folk legend. There is *János vitéz* (John the Valiant) by Sándor Petőfi (1823–49), which evokes the world of folk tales; and then there is János Arany's *Toldi*, which conjures up the world of legends.

# kings

## Csilla Bakody

Almost five hundred years divided Hungary's two greatest kings, Szent István I (Saint Stephen I; reigned 1000–38) and Mátyás Hunyadi, also known as Corvinus Mátyás and Matthias Corvinus (reigned 1458–90, and typically referred to as King Matthias in English). These two figures are, hands down, the nation's best known, most popular kings. Their names are familiar these days even to those Magyars who don't spend much time at all thinking about their country's history. Saint Stephen, known as the "founder of the [Hungarian] state," was the founding member of Hungary's first and longest lasting royal line, the Árpád dynasty. As for Matthias the Just (see also the previous chapter), he was the first Hungarian king unrelated to the Árpád dynasty even through the family's female line.

Both of these kings can safely be regarded as the most successful Hungarian leaders ever. And, indeed, their lives show some striking parallels.

Each had a father who was likewise a key figure of Hungarian history. Stephen's father, Prince Géza, promulgated Christianity in Hungary—not least, by making it obligatory. Matthias's father, János Hunyadi, was meanwhile celebrated as one of the greatest "Turk-bashing" military leaders Hungary has ever seen.

Neither Stephen nor Matthias had an easy time of it ascending to the throne. Although Stephen was chosen crown prince after Géza's death, his pagan relative, the chieftain Koppány, took up arms to acquire the throne. At stake in the struggle between Stephen and Koppány was not only the question of who would lead the Magyar people, but probably also the far-reaching matter of whether

Hungary would remain a Christian state at all. Matthias's rise to the throne, meanwhile, was preceded by two deaths. The young leader László Habsburg V accused Matthias's older brother, László Hunyadi, of treason, and had him decapitated; whereupon a plague did away with him, too. With this twist of fate, Matthias had an unimpeded path to the throne.

The development of Saint Stephen's Hungary ensued after his defeat of Koppány and the pagans. On Christmas Day in the year 1000, Stephen was crowned in Esztergom with a crown sent from Pope Sylvester II. This marked the beginning of the independent Kingdom of Hungary. Stephen understood that the Magyar people could survive only as an integral part of Christian Western Europe, and so his utmost aims were to promulgate the Christian faith, to break the back of pagan resistance, and to build up the institutions of the new state. Credit goes to him for the development and consolidation of the system of counties and the modern structure of the Hungarian Roman Catholic Church. What is more, his universal impact on the Christianity of the time is shown by the fact that he was canonized even by the Orthodox Church.

Saint Stephen I (reigned 1000–38) as depicted on a 10,000-forint banknote

It is with good reason that Hungarian historians remember King Matthias as one of our nation's great kings. The Kingdom of Hungary was strengthened under his reign, and its foreign policy was successful, too. Matthias established a celebrated mercenary force known as the Black Army, and although he engaged in battle far and wide for a good long time, he maintained order within the kingdom itself. However, he failed to realize his great dream, that of becoming Holy Roman Emperor. Matthias's reputation for being a fair-minded fellow made him a legend, and indeed it secured his place in the world of Hungarian legends. (See also the previous chapter.) After his death, a saying took root that Hungarians are apt to say even today: "Matthias has died, so much for justice." From childhood on, Máttyás was busy familiarizing himself with the century's new, humanist ideas. Under his reign Buda became a veritable bastion of Renaissance culture, with numerous Italian artists and scholars employed by the court.

King Matthias (reigned 1458–90)

Writers of the era held Matthias to be one of the century's great patrons of the arts. Matthias's historian was Bonfini. The king's library, the Bibliotheca Corviniana, which was famous throughout Europe even then, was home to a wealth of works by everyone from the authors of antiquity to the humanist writers of that era. With its approximately two thousand volumes, this library in Buda was second in size only to the Vatican library. Only some two hundred of these volumes still survive, albeit scattered among the libraries of twelve different countries.

Both Stephen and Matthias had foreign wives, and neither king had much luck when it came to producing an heir. Stephen's heir, Prince Imre—who was born of Stephen's marriage in 996 to Gizella, Princess of Bavaria—died unexpectedly in 1031; and so Hungary's first king was left without a direct descendant who could take the throne. Finally he named his nephew, Péter Orseolo, as his successor, who for his part was unable to follow through successfully on his predecessor's nation-building: inner struggles ensued, and to make matters worse, Hungary fell victim to foreign incursions.

In 1476, twelve years after the death of his first wife, Catherine Podebrad (daughter of the Czech king), Matthias married Beatrix, daughter of the King of Naples. They had no children. (See the next chapter for a possible explanation.) Matthias consequently wished to secure the throne for his illegitimate son, János Corvin. However, he failed to pull this off, and Hungary, under the Jagello dynasty, fell into anarchy.

Natural deaths were the lot of both Stephen and Matthias. Stephen died in 1038 in Székesfehérvár, where he was buried in the royal basilica he'd established there. According to chronicles, the nation mourned him for three years. As for Matthias, he died in 1490 at the age of forty-seven—in Vienna, which he had managed to occupy five years earlier. His body lay in state there, and he, too, was buried in Székesfehérvár. Public mourning lasted for three months.

The memory of each of these two great kings lives on in various ways in Hungary today. One of the oldest of Hungarian holidays, August 20, is Saint Stephen's Day—a day that also commemorates the founding of the Hungarian Christian state. Budapest's Saint Stephen Basilica was built in Stephen's memory between 1851 and 1905. Its chapel became home to one of the most important relics of the Hungarian Christian state, which had previously been kept in Vienna—namely, Saint Stephen's mummified right "hand" (actually the metacarpus.) Every August 20, the *Szent Jobb* (literally: Saint Right [Hand]) is paraded around downtown Budapest in the vicinity of the Basilica.

As for King Matthias, the Church of Our Lady on Budapest's Castle Hill, more commonly known as Matthias Church, was named after him. Although the look of the present church dates to the nineteenth century, it was in an earlier church on this site that Matthias held both of his weddings. That's not all. Matthias, who is remembered as having made his way in disguise among the common folk and dispensing justice fairly, was to become the most popular character of Hungarian folk tales and folk legends.

# queen consorts

## Szabolcs Parragh

Traditionally speaking, Hungary has imported those fine ladies who have married its kings—if possible from the West, of course, as with so many other sought-after imports. Her person may represent a pledge of peace, the hope of joining a larger power alliance, or simply an opportunity to lure foreign money, soldiers, and arms to Hungary. Love is naturally a factor rarely indeed. And, as occasionally occurs with imports, sometimes the deal goes sour. That said, as is the case with so many other aspects of our history, Hungarians' melancholic collective memory has a way of zeroing in on failures here, too.

As regards each queen consort who made a name for herself, the possibilities were invariably promising early on. The Hungarian king held by history to be the most successful, and whose figure has grown to mythical proportions more than that of any other, King Matthias (reigned 1458–90; see previous two chapters) married a woman who came from Naples. Beatrice (Beatrix) of Naples (1457–1508) was consistently described by the era's humanist scholars—Antonio Bonfini, Coelius Calcagnini, Naldus Naldius, and Galeotto Marzio—in the warmest of terms. True, perhaps they did so with a bit of compensation in mind, at least food and lodging, but they always spoke of Beatrice as a cultivated, beautiful, and virtuous woman. Could Matthias have expected anything more? And, of course, as a good homemaker, she surely did much to create the blossoming Hungarian Renaissance court.

It was on the plains beside Székesfehérvár that, on December 12, 1476, King Matthias, after twelve years as a widower, married his fiancée amid much pomp and circumstance. And, indeed, she surely deserved it. After all, a good many notable figures of contemporary Europe had sung the praises of her refinement and cultivation. The problems began only then.

One big problem was precisely the queen consort's oft-mentioned chaste virtue, whose perhaps all-too tangible consequence was that Matthias was unable to produce a legitimate male heir. Ultimately, Beatrice's predilection to frequently slip out from the embrace of her husband's loving arms by claiming a headache caused a serious power crisis—a crisis exacerbated by the fact that the virtuous betrothed also coveted the throne. Indeed, she even received theoretical support for this cause from her faithful humanists. Bonfini, in one of his books dedicated to Beatrice (*Symposion de virgintate et pudicitia coniugali—Discussion of Virginity and on the Purity of Conjugal Life*, c. 1485), did much to show that that Beatrice's chastity only went to prove that—in the event of her husband's death, of course—power should go to this clever and pretty, but bodily unassailable queen.

Hungarian noblemen, who were less familiar with this sort of platonic metaphysics, did not exactly concur. In one of his famous historical works (*Rerum Ungarorum Decades—Decades of Hungarian History*; 1488–97), Bonfini already makes mention of Hungarians' insensitivity to matters of mind and spirit. And yet he endeavors to objectivity as he writes of what has changed in the Hungarian court since Beatrice's arrival: the court's uncouth, albeit puritan and disciplined circumstances had been supplanted by a highborn, opulent lifestyle. True, "the Hungarians were unfamiliar with high culture and pleasures." While something was invariably lost, the sheer wealth of the new warmed the cockles of the humanist heart.

A century on, the Hungarian translator of Bonfini's work, Gáspár Heltai, rewrites Bonfini's lines in what sounds a whole lot more like complaining (Hung.: *Krónika a Magyarok Dolgairól—Chronicle of Hungarian Affairs*; 1575): Matthias's court was filled to the brims with scholars, with learned men, but let us not forget that they received "incalculable recompense every month." Indeed, even that era's businessman feared the effect on the court's budget of all these cultivated ne'er-do-wells who had been lured to this country in part by the queen's reputation. And, of course, Heltai and his contemporaries also had to explain how it was that, within a couple decades of the death of that great (and just) king, the country had well-nigh collapsed and fell mostly under Turkish occupation. Their answer: the blame was due at least in part to his queen, that poor scapegoat who had not only turned Hungarians into wimps but also couldn't even manage to give the nation a male heir.

Although it is difficult to assess the legitimacy of all these emotions, it is a fact that Beatrice did take her part in the succession-related feuds that followed Matthias's death. In the skirmishing between Matthias's illegitimate son, János Corvin, and Ulászló she sided with the latter. Indeed, she even got him to take her as his wife, although this new husband of hers, who was in fact soon chosen king, never was willing to recognize the marriage. And so Beatrice finally returned to Italy, from where she sued for her dowry, and she died alone in the court in 1508. Hungarians have been left with the memory of a foreign queen consort who yearned for power. Over in Naples, meanwhile, it is perhaps tradition to remember the ups and downs in the life of a refined young lady whose lot it was to have an extended sojourn in the land of the barbarians.

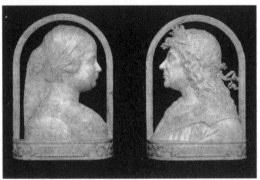

Beatrice of Naples (1457–1508)
& King Matthias (reigned 1458–90)

# saints

## Csilla Bakody

Hungary's Chapel of Our Lady at Saint Peter's Basilica in the Vatican is usually closed to visitors. However, those fortunate pilgrims who manage to get in on a Tuesday morning for Holy Mass can see reliefs depicting beatified and canonized Hungarians. The veneration of saints is among the most important aspects of Christianity, and the aim of canonization and beatification is to provide the world with exemplars whose lives offer special help to many in making ethical decisions and forming values. But just who are these blessed souls?

There is a long line of Hungarian saints and beatified souls. Quite a few of them were recognized as such by the Vatican without any request having been made by the Hungarian Church. The first canonization of a Hungarian happened in 1083, when the honor went to no less than five persons: Stephen I, Imre, and Gellért, as well as the two hermits of Zobor (formerly in northern Hungary, today in present-day Slovakia), Zoerard-András and Benedek. One group of Hungarian saints consists of those relatively well-known figures who have their own holidays, whereas those in the other group are commemorated collectively on November 13. Together, the nation's saints and beatified souls are a motley bunch. Some weren't even of Hungarian descent, but achieved their posthumous status owing to their deeds in Hungary; for example, Saint Gellért (a propagator of Christianity), the Venetian-born monk Gerard Sagredo who was stabbed to death with a lance by pagans in 1046; Saint John of Capistrano (protector of Christianity and the patron of jurists), who died in Ilok, Hungary, three months after marching at the head of 70,000 Christians at a great victory over the Turks;

Gizella the Blessed (Hungarian queen and wife of Saint Stephen); and Károly IV the Blessed (Hungary's last king).

And then there are those, indeed there are more of them, who, although they were Hungarian by birth, made their names by serving other peoples. Among them are Saint Elizabeth of the Árpád dynasty, who served the poor; Saint Hedvig, Queen of Poland; Saint Kinga, a Franciscan Clarissa nun in Poland; and Saint Piroska (*Piroska* being her given name before she was married off to the Byzantine Emperor; *Irene Prisca* as known by the Greek Orthodox Church, which canonized her).

The third group comprises those Hungarians who earned their distinction through deeds performed at home. Those in this group are perhaps closest to the hearts of Hungarians today: Saint Stephen

Saint Margit (1242–70)

(founder of the Hungarian state and builder of Hungary's church), Saint Imre (Saint Stephen's son, patron saint of Hungary's youth), Saint László (the Knight-King), Saint Margit (daughter of King Béla IV and martyr of penance). As for beatified souls in this third group, they include Özséb the Blessed, founder of the only Hungarian religious order, the Pálos Order; Vilmos Apor the Blessed, Bishop of Győr and a martyr; and László Batthyány-Strattmann the Blessed, the nineteenth-century physician whose expertise in opthamology and providing of free services to those who couldn't pay earned him the sobriquets "eye doctor" and "doctor to the poor."

As for their family lineage, perhaps it needn't come as a surprise that all of Hungary's saints and beatified souls—with the exception of László Batthány-Strattmann, who was nonetheless of noble birth—have derived from royalty. Indicative of the enormous prestige enjoyed in their times by Hungary's royal dynasties and of their crucial history-shaping role, the nation's first and longest-lasting royal line, the Árpád dynasty, lays claim to no less than eleven out of Hungary's twenty saints.

Naturally there are typical, defining elements of the lives of saints, such as: converting others to Christianity; building and protecting the Church; the heroic exercise of Christian virtues; a sensitivity to social causes; penance and, yes, self-discipline. Hungarian saints and beatified souls are certainly believed by believers to have displayed their share of such personal qualities and virtues.

Efforts by the Hungarian Roman Catholic Church for the Holy See to honor yet more saintly Hungarians bore fruit most recently in 2009 with the beatification of Bishop Zoltán Meszlényi. The man who took over for Archbishop József Mindszenty, Hungary's primate during a crucial period in the nation's twentieth-century history, after Mindszenty's imprisonment by the communists, was himself tortured to death by the state in 1951. The twentieth-eighth Hungarian to be called "Blessed" by the Vatican, he was preceded in 2006 by Sister Sára Salkaházi, who rescued numerous Jews during the Holocaust and was murdered in December 1944 by the fascists. The cases for the beatification of two others—Mindszenty and Áron Márton, the Bishop of Transylvania during the darkest decades of communist Romania—have meanwhile long passed beyond the labor-intensive research stage to back up their cases. Stay tuned.

# 19<sup>th</sup>-century statesmen

## Csilla Bakody

Among the most dynamic periods of Hungarian history was the Age of Reform (1830–48), which saw the blossoming of a political movement that aimed to modernize Hungary's feudal system. The reforms at issue were debated from 1825 on at national assemblies, with the first real achievements realized by the Diet of 1832–36. This particular national assembly was of special significance also because it brought together, for the first time, the century's three most important Hungarian statesmen: István Széchenyi (1791–1860), Lajos Kossuth (1802–94), and Ferenc Deák (1803–76).

Only Széchenyi's name was well known going into this national assembly, an event that gave Kossuth and Deák their first opportunity to step on the political stage. Kossuth, as a deputy representing members of the upper nobility who were absent from parliamentary sessions, occupied a seat in the Lower House; while Deák was standing in for his older brother, who had taken ill. Soon, however, both joined Széchenyi as leading figures of Hungarian political life.

While their individual political careers achieved their summits at different periods, the destinies of these three men intertwined tightly in 1848, when they all became members of Hungary's first independent government. In the government led by Lajos Batthyány, Széchenyi accepted the position of Minister of Transportation and Public Works; while Kossuth became Minister of Finance; and Deák, Minister of Justice.

This era of Hungarian history was one brimming with hope and confidence. None of these three leaders then suspected that some day István Széchenyi would be known as the "greatest Hungarian"; Ferenc Deák would be called the "nation's sage"; and that, in the collective memory of the Hungarian people, Lajos Kossuth would come to embody, more than anyone else, the 1848–49 war of independence. Nor did they suspect that Széchenyi would take his own life in 1860 in a mental institution near Vienna, where he ended up in September 1848 with a nervous breakdown. Kossuth was to die in Torino after forty-five years of exile; and Deák would live out his entire life without a family. Where did these three statesmen come from, and where did they end up?

István Széchenyi, the "greatest Hungarian," was born to a Roman Catholic, large-estate–holding family of the upper nobility. For his part, Lajos Kossuth, the "hermit of Turino," was of the Lutheran, lesser nobility with no land to its name. And Ferenc Deák, the "nation's sage," derived from an age-old aristocratic family. Kossuth and Deák studied law and both passed their bar exams. Széchenyi, like all aristocrats, was tutored at home, and following a seventeen-year military career he retired from the service in 1826 with the rank of captain.

The apex of Széchenyi's career was in the 1830s, which is when this class-conscious aristocrat who'd devoted so much of his life to the Austrian empire became a reformer committed to the future of the Hungarian nation. This was when he published his most influential books—*Hitel* (Credit, 1830), *Világ* (Light, 1831), and *Stádium* (Stage, 1832)—which spelled out his grand plans for economic reform. During this period he focused his attention on the establishment of the National Casino (an institution loftier and less gambling-oriented than your average Las Vegas casino); on massive projects to regulate the Danube and Tisza rivers; on the establishment of steamboat traffic on the Danube and on Lake Balaton; on the building of what was to become Budapest's most iconic bridge, the Chain Bridge; and on formally establishing the sport of horse racing in Hungary.

Kossuth's star shined, above all, during the revolution that erupted on March 15, 1848, and that lasted through most of the following year. The victorious military campaign of spring 1849 allowed the Hungarian national assembly to declare—on April 14, 1849, at its session in Debrecen—the dethronement of the House of Habsburg. Kossuth himself was chosen as regent and president, and until his resignation on August 11 he did in fact see to the responsibilities of head of state.

Deák retired from public life during the years of oppression that followed the failed war of independence, and re-emerged only in 1860. It was under his leadership that Hungary tied its historic Compromise with the Austrians in 1867. Although this occasion marked the peak of his career as a statesman, Deák opted against taking part in the new Hungarian government. Instead he nominated Count Gyula Andrássy as prime minister. Although he did wield a great deal of power as a party leader, after the Compromise Deák rejected every honor and title that came his way, suggesting that it wasn't personal ambition that motivated him.

These three statesmen didn't exactly agree on everything. During the 1840s Széchenyi never ceased devoting anxious attention to Kossuth's political endeavors. The more his popularity grew, the more boldly Kossuth expressed his demands in the newspaper he edited, *Pesti Hírlap*—and the more worried Széchenyi became. Concerned about the risk of revolution, Széchenyi wrote his work *Kelet népe* (People of the East), in which he outlined where the political direction espoused by Kossuth whom Széchenyi saw as a fomenter of revolution—would lead the nation.

By contrast, in the 1850s Széchenyi regarded Deák as the only Hungarian statesman capable of putting Hungary's long-term destiny in order. Kossuth, who quarreled with Deák over the 1867 Compromise, accused Deák in his *Kasszandra-levél* (Cassandra Letter), which he wrote from exile, of abandoning the cause of Hungarian independence. For his part, Deák argued that no other peaceful solution was possible; that an independent Hungary would be unsustainable without the monarchy, wedged as it would be between the Russian and German empires.

The sensitive and brilliant István Széchenyi, the fiery and passionate Lajos Kossuth, and the sagacious, calm, and collected Ferenc Deák were among the greatest figures in Hungarian history. What would they have been capable of in less trying political circumstances, had they stuck together?

István Széchenyi, the "greatest Hungarian," (1791–1860)

Ferenc Deák (1803–76)

Lajos Kossuth (1802–94)

# 20ᵗʰ-century rulers

## Ádám Masát

In Hungary, the twentieth century was that of aged rulers. Indeed, three "old men" defined the nation's main political orientation for most of the century. There was Francis Joseph I (1830–1916), born to the House of Habsburg-Lotharingen, who took the throne of the empire at the age of eighteen. Then there was Miklós Horthy (1868–1957), born in Kenderes, Hungary, to a landowning family with a medium-size estate. And, most recently, there was János Kádár (1912–89), whose birth certificate, reflecting the fact that he was an illegitimate child, featured his mother's family name, Csermanek. (He took on the name Kádár only in 1945, in line with the fashion of dropping foreign-sounding names in favor of typical, generic Magyar ones.)

Famous for his stately beard and military demeanor, Francis Joseph lived eighty-six years. Horthy, known for the large, sailor's tatoo on his arm and for his admiral's uniform, died at eighty-nine. And Kádár, who donned a red kerchief when in the company of young pioneers, but who usually wore a grey suit that better matched his personality, made it to seventy-seven.

Of the three, Francis Joseph least embodied the twentieth-century ruler. This is not surprising, given that he passed the bulk of his life in the nineteenth century, and that politics for him was not a matter of choice: ancestry had predestined him for the role of being Hungary's head of state. All the same, the names of each of these three leaders became inseparable from their particular historic eras: that of Francis Joseph with the Age of Dualism that followed the Austro-Hungarian Compromise of 1867; Horthy's,

138

with the period between the First and Second World Wars; and Kádár's, with those decades of the communist era that stretched from the 1956 revolution to the collapse of one-party rule more than three decades later (although Kádár himself died shortly before this came to pass).

All three rulers occupied the top posts of very different political regimes. Francis Joseph was Emperor from 1848 until 1916; and, from 1867, the year of the great Austro-Hungarian Compromise, he was also recognized as King of Hungary. Horthy, who for his part was regent of Hungary (1920–44), had vast powers at his disposal in a political system that can, with little exaggeration, be termed a kingdom without a king. As for Kádár, he led Hungary (1956–88) as First Secretary of the communist party in a Soviet-style dictatorship. All three rose to power after a watershed historical event: Francis Joseph, during the 1848–49 Hungarian war of independence; Horthy, following the short-lived revolutions after World War I; and Kádár, with the 1956 revolution.

All three began their reigns with a period of severe political oppression. Francis Joseph, barely a young man at the time, introduced himself to Hungarians, as it were, with the execution of thirteen Hungarian generals at Arad in 1849. Horthy's ascent to power in 1919 was accompanied by the so-called White Terror; and to say the least, Kádár also made quite a name for himself in pursuing harsh oppression. Foreign military intervention helped seal the power of all three. The Habsburg ruler crushed Hungary's struggle for independence with the help of the Russian czar. The invasion of Hungary by Romanian troops after World War I played a major role in the failure of the communist Council Republic, and this paved the way for Horthy to take control. And without Soviet military intervention, breaking the back of the 1956 revolution would have been impossible.

*"I have considered everything, I have thought over everything."* Posters bearing these words with the signature of Francis Joseph appeared on the streets of Budapest in 1914 when he sent his

troops into battle. Although he didn't live out the war, soon before his death Francis Joseph must have suspected that he'd made a great mistake. Not only did the Monarchy lose the war, but the war cast a shadow over his life's work: his multiethnic empire fell to pieces on June 28, 1919, with the Treaty of Versailles.

*"Here and now, on the bank of the Danube, I call the Hungarian capital to judgment."* These were Horthy's words of challenge to a Budapest that had *"dressed in red rags"* under the reign of the communist Council Republic (March 21, 1919–August 1, 1919) on Gellért Square as he rode into town on November 16, 1919. As regent he held "revisionism"—that is, the reinstatement of Hungary's pre-1920, pre–Treaty of Trianon borders—to be his foremost foreign policy objective. Although he didn't care for Hitler, through most of his reign Horthy followed a pro-German foreign policy and, indeed, he signed anti-Jewish laws. Even after German forces occupied Hungary, though, Horthy managed to bring a short-lived halt to the deportation of Jews; this, despite his ill-fated subsequent attempt to pull the country out of World War II. By kidnapping his son, the Germans forced Horthy to resign and hand over the reigns of power to the fascists.

*"He who isn't against us is with us!"* Kádár's motto rang loud and clear when first voiced in 1961, signaling his wish to establish a gentler dictatorship than that of his brutal predecessor, Mátyás Rákosi. During the 1956 revolution, Kádár sided with the Soviets, and on returning to Hungary from Moscow he declared the establishment of the Hungarian Revolutionary Workers-Peasant Government, of which he became prime minister. Until May 1988 he remained at the helm of the Hungarian Socialist Workers Party, and through much of this time he endeavored to legitimize his soft dictatorship with a gradual betterment of living standards and by international recognition on the foreign policy front. Integral to Kádár's rule was his endeavor to exploit perceived limits to the utmost in every area of life. He continuously slackened rigid constraints in the realms of politics, economics,

culture, and science. Effectively speaking, until the crisis of the 1980s Kádár carried out his reform-laden liberalization policy with notable success—in East Bloc terms, that is. He didn't live to see the collapse of the regime he had sought to sustain. But his own comrades stripped him of power. And, in a twist of fate, he died on July 6, 1989—the very day that Hungary's prime minister during the 1956 revolution, Imre Nagy, whose execution Kádár had conspired in, was officially rehabilitated.

Had Hungary's three major twentieth-century rulers not lived as long as they did, perhaps history would look upon them differently. Had Francis Joseph died around the turn of the twentieth century, as the man who had held together a multiethnic empire, he would have entered Hungary's history books as the king of the "balmy days of peace." Had Horthy not been around for the most shameful circumstances of his reign—the terrors that ensued in Hungary in the first half of the 1940s, including the deportation of Jews, not to mention the anti-Jewish laws that got underway earlier; the annihilation of the Second Hungarian Army; and the country's occupation by German forces—today he would perhaps be remembered primarily for the substantial social and cultural development that unfolded in Hungary in the 1920s and 1930s. Had Kádár kicked the bucket in the early 1980s, before Hungary fell headlong into an economic-political crisis that finally brought the regime to its knees, Hungarians might have remembered him primarily as the creator of "goulash communism"—as the man who made it possible for Hungary to be the "merriest barrack" in the Soviet camp during the communist era.

But this is what happened: The father of the Monarchy led Hungary headlong into World War I, which resulted not only in the empire's destruction but in Hungary's traumatic loss of two-thirds of its territory under the 1920 Treaty of Trianon. As for Horthy, that equestrian-cum-admiral gave space to right-wing forces on Hungary's political spectrum and allowed his country to be swept into the catastrophic finality of World War II—a war there was no way of emerging from victoriously. And the communist party's eminently grey soldier was powerless to stop our nation's spiraling trail into debt. Indeed, he led us firmly into an economic crisis— one from which neither further reforms, nor a different approach to the one-party system, promised a way out.

And then, a decade before the century came to a close, there came a brave new era of multiparty democracy. Hungarians could at last look freely into the past, and decide for themselves just how to remember the nation's three most influential twentieth-century rulers—men who carved out for themselves ambivalent reputations indeed.

Francis Joseph I (1830–1916)

Miklós Horthy (1868–1957)

János Kádár (1912–89)

# porcelain

## Orsolya Nádor

Those nations of the world where a distinguished porcelain manufacturing tradition has developed over the centuries are invariably as proud as can be of their achievements on this front. We need only think of all the fine plates, vases, and tableware that has come from China; from the Germany city of Meissen, on the Elbe; from Delft, in the western Netherlands; from Vienna; and, last but not least, from Herend, Hungary.

No serious porcelain collection is complete without a Herend, as all Hungarians would readily agree.

Centuries before porcelain began making its way around Europe, Hungary's geographical attributes made it possible for pottery works to emerge in notable fashion in various parts of the country. These facilities provided households with water jugs and milk jugs, small earthenware pots, and other such indispensable objects. In the first third of the nineteenth century there arose out of this tradition small manufacturing facilities specializing in porcelain, and some of these were to become full-fledged factories. Let us now look at the three most illustrious among them: those in Herend, Pécs, and Hollóháza.

Herend, a village west of the Danube, has been manufacturing stoneware since 1826 and unique, finely crafted porcelain since 1839. In its early period, under the direction of Mór Fischer, the facility modeled its products after Chinese porcelain; indeed, it managed to produce pieces that were spitting images of bona fide, Chinese china. Although Herend still lays claim to some designs of this sort, it soon developed a style all its own, with a fine, diaphanous, snow-white base and characteristic, hand-painted principal motifs: butterflies, flowers, and fruit. Some such designs bear the names of the famous families that commissioned them; for example, the Apponyi design. Beginning in 1896, Herend began producing its characteristically Hungarian statuettes—from the young lad and a young woman in the colorful folk costume of the Matyó region (near Mezőkövesd, in eastern Hungary), to the herdsman, to endearing animal figurines. And then came more artistic statues, such as the veiled female dancer. Herend porcelain, which developed from a centuries-old artisans' technique, never was exactly for budget-minded shoppers. Large orders were placed by ruling families, leading church figures, and upper-crust nobility; and, later, in the communist era and beyond, by leading "comrades" and newly moneyed businessmen. Hungarians typically give Herend porcelain as gifts only on the most special occasions; for example, at weddings. Virtually every self-respecting Magyar household has one or two Herend statuettes, a Herend pastry service, a Herend coffee cup, or a Herend vase; for the most part, relics of Grandmother's younger days.

On now to the lovely southern city of Pécs—more specifically, to the Zsolnay factory, which gained fame for its singular porcelain-manufacturing process. Vilmos Zsolnay gets the credit for having expanded the business from a small manufacturing facility into a large-scale enterprise producing a varied array of state-of-the-art porcelain. One characteristic attribute of Zsolnay vases, tableware, and ornamental objects is their quill-painted, rich array of thin, delicate lines on an ivory background; these portray butterflies, cornflowers, or Persian designs. One of the Zsolnay plant's most closely guarded secrets is its unique, golden-hued green or wine-red "eosin" glaze, which it developed in the 1890s. To some collectors, this glaze is synonymous with the very word "Zsolnay." A stroll around Budapest, Pécs, or Kecskemét reveals numerous buildings with colorful, mosaic-like roofs that bring to mind the best of Zsolnay. Indeed, one of the most characteristic styles of Hungarian art nouveau ornamentation for buildings was "pyrogranite," which endures all sorts of weather and carries on the reputation of the Zsolnay works.

In addition to these two world-famous centers of porcelain manufacturing, several smaller facilities opened in their wake to produce fine earthenware. For example, a facility in the village of Városlőd, near Herend, produced thick, glazed earthenware for a far wider spectrum of village and urban households than did Herend; while another facility, in the town of Hódmezővásárhely, specialized in earthenware with a green background; and yet another, in the village of Nádudvar, came to be known for its black ornamental objects.

The porcelain of Hollóháza, a village in the hilly, forested northeast corner of present-day Hungary, is roughly as old as that of Herend or Pécs, but for decades it served a different purpose. Practically every nineteenth- and twentieth-century Hungarian household had its share of Hollóháza jugs, jars, mugs, and plates used for everyday meals. These typically featured blue and red floral motifs on a white background. Since this factory manufactured products for consumers with modest pocketbooks, its technology reflected this: designs were not painted by hand, but were instead the product of die-casting and stenciling. The facility achieved real distinction and international notoriety only when an innovative Hungarian painter, Endre Szász (1923–2003), dissatisfied with having his work appear only on paper, dreamed of his paintings appearing on porcelain. A cooperative effort yielded beautiful coffee- and tea-sets, ornamental objects, and enormous paintings that occupy entire walls. Every single such object is numbered, and each was bestowed with the artist's signature before leaving the factory.

There are few things more celebrated *and* more quintessentially Hungarian, as we Magyars see it, than Hungarian porcelain. Indeed, even this realm of our nation's art, which is otherwise spoken of in such polished terms, has not escaped the humor typical of Hungarian sayings. When someone behaves a tad insensitively or crudely in a delicate situation, a Hungarian may well remark that he or she is acting *"mint egy elefánt a porcelánboltban."* While this translates literally as "like an elephant in a porcelain shop," it does sound an awful lot like what English speakers know well as "like a bull in a china shop," doesn't it? The moral of the story: Hungarian porcelain may be truly Hungarian, but porcelain is truly international.

# appetizers & desserts

## Nóra Csontos

One thing alone links the appetizer with the dessert: the main course. This is like s–. (Here we might muse upon another source of human pleasure, but best leave that for another place, another book, another writer.) So then, eating—otherwise known as gastronomic pleasure—begins with the appetizer and closes with the dessert.

Let's begin our look at this aspect of Hungarian gastronomy with the *palacsinta*! Our appetizer will be *hortobágyi palacsinta*; our dessert, *Gundel-palacsinta*. The *palacsinta*—Hungary's version of the crepe—is salty when served as an appetizer, sweet when called upon to please the palate as a dessert. The *hortobágyi palacsinta*—which gets its name from Hungary's greatest great plain, the Hortobágy—is filled with chicken paprikash cooked (to the point where the chicken crumbles) and then ground before being stuffed into the thin, round sheet of cooked pastry—which, unlike the dessert version of the *palacsinta*, is then folded up into a plump square of sorts. Finally, the whole thing is topped off with a liberal dash of sour cream and perhaps a sprinkling of paprika.

The *Gundel palacsinta*—which got its name from Károly Gundel, one of the most famous of all Hungarian gastronomists—is filled with a blend of ground walnuts and sugar cooked in a little milk, and rendered all the more irresistible with some candied orange peels and one or more considered spoonfuls of rum. Once we have all this wrapped up, while still hot we top it off with a thick, likewise hot, chocolate sauce laced with, yes, just a little more rum—and it's ready to serve.

As long as we're on the subject of the *palacsinta*, let's see what else Hungarians are inclined to fill it with: jam, sweet cocoa powder, sweet pudding, chopped stewed fruit, cinnamon-flavored sugar; and, last but not least, a special concoction using *édes túró* (sweet curd), which is perhaps truly, singularly, strangely Hungarian. Here it might be noted that curd cheese made from cow's milk is that staple ingredient of ours which, in foreign eyes, makes us seem by turns like real gourmets or else like queer fish indeed.

Making the sweet-curd filling for the palacsinta and for various other Hungarian pastries is simplicity itself, as long as you are able to buy some curd—next to impossible, in America—or have a generous cow in your barn. Here's how: Beat some curd and sour cream to a froth with sugar and/or vanilla-flavored sugar. Some housewives mix in an egg yolk, too. A bit of grated lemon rind imparts an exquisite tanginess to the mixture. We might also throw in a handful of raisins and or chopped peaches or other fruit. Sweet-curd filling often ends up in our famous, thin, nay, virtually translucent *rétes* (strudel) dough; and, when it does, some people are fond of adding a bit of grated, lightly salted squash. And no discussion of what sweet-curd means to Hungarians would be complete without mentioning the *Turó Rudi*—that chocolate-covered, sausage-shaped confection so many of us simply can't resist plucking off the shelf in the refrigerated dairy products section of the supermarket. Originally a Soviet sweet, the *Turó Rudi* failed to achieve real popularity only where it came from, the USSR— perhaps owing to its unusual combination of flavors. The *Turó Rudi* was first manufactured in Hungary using sausage-stuffing machines and was packaged by hand. But in no time it was such a hit with consumers that its producers soon adopted a more efficient, industrial manufacturing technique.

Curd and sour cream—these two dairy products that are such staple ingredients in the Hungarian kitchen—can also be used to make salted appetizers.

Take *körözött*, for example. In addition to the two above-mentioned ingredients, this one-of-a-kind, spiced spread is also heavy on sweet paprika—an ingredient that can safely be called truly Hungarian. This is not to mention caraway seeds, salt, finely chopped onions, and a bit of mustard or garlic depending on taste. The whole concoction is then whipped to a thick froth before being served with bread. That said, few sights impress guests more than *körözött*-filled, slender, green Hungarian peppers—peppers that are then sliced and typically served on a cold plate brimming with a colorful array of other appetizers. Or they might be served directly to our individual plates. What *are* these other appetizers? They can be many, of course, but here's one that's sure to please most Magyar mouths: cold goose-liver served with bread that's been spread with goose fat and thinly sliced red onions.

New York Café, Budapest, at the turn of the twentieth century

Once we've had our fill of all these filling appetizers and even more filling main courses, what in the way of *light* desserts might we turn to, so as to feel less stuffed? *Hmm. Mm.* There is the justifiably popular *Somlói galuska*. One day long ago, Károly Gollerits, head waiter at Budapest's fabled Gundel Restaurant, decided to pour a heap of vanilla cream over some chocolate-flavored or plain *piskótagaluska* (small cubes of sponge cake). He sprinkled the result with roughly chopped walnuts, and served it with chocolate sauce and whipped cream. He named the heavenly dessert after his wife's birthplace, *Somló-hegy*.

Another one of Károly Gundel's cuisine creations was *kecskeméti barackpuding* (Peach Pudding à la Kecskemét), which got its name from the famous *pálinka* (peach brandy) produced in the city of Kecskemét, central Hungary—that super-strong spirit that positively smacks of bona fide Hungarian flavor. In short, this particular brand of *pálinka* is mixed into the peach pudding, and the result is served with fresh peaches.

*Dobos-torta* (Dobos cake), named after its creator, master confectioner József C. Dobos, is unique not only because its top consists of a one-of-a-kind, toasted, sugary glaze, but also because the icing between the cake's many thin layers is made with slightly salted butter.

And, yes, there is the ubiquitous *rétes* (strudel), made from that previously mentioned, virtually translucent, thin dough and packed with a good many different sorts of filling (which in almost all cases are sugary-sweet): just plain sweet-curd, sweet curd with chopped dill mixed in, or sweet curd blended with finely grated squash; a sugary mash of poppy seeds, sometimes mixed with finely grated squash; slightly salted, shredded cabbage; sweetened-stewed sour cherries; or sweetened-stewed chopped apples.

This is not to mention a good many other delicious desserts. But do beware: even main courses in Hungary can be scrumptious, so before devouring what's put in front of you, consider that a typical Magyar meal comprises at least three courses—each of which stands ready to fill you to the hilt if you're not careful! So let's make good use of what free space remains in our bellies. After all, it would be a shame to leave out any course.

# food

## Nóra Csontos

What must we take into account if want what we eat to be truly Hungarian? Simple: heavy on the onions, plenty of paprika, and, ideally, spicy. And, with that, we've pretty much defined the essence of Hungarian *gulyás*, which is thus poised for inclusion on UNESCO's World Heritage list—or, well, in an ideal world it would be.

No Hungarian meal worth its salt is complete without three core ingredients: onions, paprika, and lard. And where these ingredients come from does matter: the onions must be (or at least *said* to be) from Makó, that small town on the plains of eastern Hungary that has cultivated the nation's finest onions since the nineteenth century; the paprika, ground from the treasured red peppers of Szeged or Kalocsa; and the lard, which just has to be bona fide pork lard! As for the last of these staples, this is how one essential aspect of a Hungarian recipe would have read almost until the end of the twentieth century. By then, however, a new strain of gastronomic thinking—*reformkonyha* (healthy cuisine)—had registered its effect at least to some degree in most Hungarian households. These days, the vast majority of Hungarians use not lard but vegetable oil; and, if possible, oil low in saturated fats. And on taking the lid off that pot on the range or opening the oven, we are much more likely nowadays to find not fat-rich meats but poultry. But just because most modern-day Magyars forego traditional ingredients in cooking, many a family does still have a soft spot in their hearts for truly Hungarian foods. So let us see what we can make using the three basic ingredients above.

*Gulyás.* Beyond the three core ingredients, this thick stew requires cubes of beef or pork. (Never poultry, mind you, for there's no such thing as health-food *gulyás!*) Add a little water to the pot, as well as or, better yet, wine. The meat stews in this mixture for several hours. Making it in a bona fide stew-kettle, with plenty of fresh air, over a smoldering wood fire can't hurt, either; for, indeed, truly Hungarian gulyás is cooked in the great outdoors. What we make with the same ingredients, but indoors, is called *pörkölt*.

*Gulyás* is used to make *gulyásleves* (goulash soup—i.e., what "Hungarian goulash" often refers to in English). To the gulyás we add vegetables, plenty of water, and thin strips of dough called *csipetke* (made of water, eggs, flour, and a dash of salt, and plucked in tiny pieces right into the boiling water). *Gulyás* or *pörkölt* can also be used to make *palócleves* (Palóc Soup): after adding water we mix in enough sour cream to thicken the soup, flavor it with tarragon, and just before removing the pot from the fire or the range we add a little vinegar. If we do make *gulyás* with chicken, then it's not called *gulyás* at all, but *csirkepörkölt* (aka *paprikáscsirke* or *csirkepaprikás*)—known to the world as *chicken paprikash*. To this, we typically add a hearty dash of sour cream—and what would it be without a plateful of cucumber salad?!

The three basic ingredients can also be used to make "vegetarian" Hungarian foods. (Of course, since these foods would, traditionally speaking, contain lard, serious vegetarians would beg to differ; but such is the typical interpretation of vegetarianism in Hungary.) For example, *lecsó*—whose ever-present summertime aroma pervades so many apartment-house stairwells and countryside yards. This savory smell begins taking shape when chopped onions and bits of bacon are fried to a golden brown in lard, followed by sliced tomatoes and peppers thrown on top and boiled to the consistency of a thick stew; and spiced with, yes, paprika! More often than not, Hungarians can't resist adding an egg or two or else some sausage to the mix—despite the fact that doing so further calls into question the already dubious vegetarian credentials of *lecsó*. An even simpler, highly economical alternative is *paprikás krumpli* (potato paprikash), which sees simply crumbled, boiled potatoes mixed into the lard-fried onions. Bits of sausage often enter the picture here as well.

Fish, too, can be used to make *pörkölt*. The result: *halpaprikás* (fish paprikash). If we add enough water to turn it into a soup, it becomes *halászlé* (fish soup). Depending on the particular region of Hungary whose gastronomic traditions are being adhered to, this can be either thick or thin, with lots of fish or just a little, with *csipetke* plucked in or without.

We Hungarians have yet more strange dining habits where these came from. For example, instead of a traditional appetizer we often begin our meals with a particularly substantial "appetizer stand-in," one that often also suffices as a main course—such as *bableves csülökkel* (bean soup with knuckle of pork) and *pörkölt* served with *túrós csusza* (curd heaped on top of a boiled, noodle-like pastry that rather resembles shredded paper).

Yet another main course that often finds its way to Hungarian dinner tables and, indeed, makes for a popular, economical lunch is *fôzelék* (a thick, usually salty, vegetable stew). This is well outside the realm of *pörkölt* and *gulyás*, of course, except for the fact that—again, traditionally speaking—it often starts out with lard. *Fôzelék* comprises a single vegetable—whether string beans, squash, potatoes, cabbage, or lentils—boiled in water, flavored (with salt and perhaps dill, for example), and whipped with sour cream or thickened with *rántás* (i.e., roux, which, in contemporary Hungarian cooking, is a bit of wheat flour fried in oil or lard). Usually it's served with a so-called *feltét* (cover)—such as *fasírt* (a meatloaf patty) or fried pork—but sometimes (the more economical, more vegetarian alternative) only with a thick slice of fresh bread. Those waist-conscious connoisseurs out to lose some kilos can have it as is, minus even the bread.

Now that we know the essentials of Hungarian cuisine, all that's left for us to do is sample all of this—ideally, in a charming little garden restaurant and at a table with a checkered tablecloth.

# spices

István Bori

*Habeat colorem, odorem, et saporem.* So goes a Latin saying about wine. That is: May it have color, bouquet, and zest. This can also be said of foods—which, when prepared in "Hungarian" fashion, have two core ingredients that concern themselves with producing such desired effects: paprika and the common onion. Hungarian cuisine has a reputation as being decidedly spicy, with heavy foods filling the menu. But if they, if *we*, only knew. . . . Back in the olden days, centuries ago, Hungarian housewives and the chefs employed by aristocratic families used many more spices than they do today. Rosemary, ginger, tarragon, and a whole host of other spices have all but vanished from Hungarian kitchens, and have only recently begun to reappear. Similarly, few Hungarians actually use the various forms of paprika that are available. Hot or nonbiting, sweet or semisweet, finely ground or not so finely ground varieties each represent a different category of taste.

Paprika has been known in Hungary since the sixteenth century, and indeed its alternative name *törökbors* (Turkish pepper) alludes to the fact that the Turks brought it here. For a long time it was used primarily not even as a spice but, rather, as a medicine reputed to have various beneficial properties. Peasants living amid the swampy plains of eastern Hungary treated malaria with paprika-"crazed" *pálinka* (fruit bandy)—a drink that, back then, was typically consumed for its perceived health benefits. (See the next chapter for more on *pálinka*.)

At the end of the nineteenth century, paprika was used to make an antirheumatism ointment. Its use as a spice dates back to the eighteenth century, and since the nineteenth century it has been cultivated traditionally in two regions, near Szeged and near Kalocsa. Paprika became a leading export product in the twentieth century. Storm clouds are gathering on the export front at the start of the twenty-first century, however. Increasingly, the requisite peppers we manage to produce domestically are insufficient in supply to provide the raw material that's needed for our own households to be well endowed with our world-renowned "Hungarian" paprika; and so we must import to round out the supply. On the other hand, to produce the wide array of paprika-containing products ubiquitous on Hungarian supermarket shelves—from spice mixes and soup cubes, as well as relishes and spreads that come in jars and tubes— traditional manufacturing techniques must be complemented by paprika that's often laced to the hilt with artificial flavors and colors; and imported paprika often doesn't suffice in this respect. Such products carry such colorful names as *Erôs Pista* (Strong-Spicy-Hot Pista; complete with a mustachioed old timer, Pista, on the label) and *Édes Anna* ("Sweet" Anna; an allusion to the title character of a classic, early twentieth-century novel by this title).

In short, even Hungary's most iconic vegetable product might be at risk. But allow me to ease the reader's fears: bona fide Hungarian paprika can't disappear, after all, for what would *gulyásleves* or *pörkölt* (see previous chapter) look like in a yellowish sauce?

And what would such foods be without the onion? The onion is among Hungary's oldest cultivated food plants. Its reputation in Hungary has long become intertwined with a small town in the southern reaches of the eastern plains, Makó. Ever since the nineteenth century this town has had a street-full of onion growers. Initially they were poverty-stricken peasants forced by frequent flooding to give up grape-growing and opt instead for the exceptionally labor-intensive task of onion cultivation. Obviously there were such folk elsewhere in Hungary, too. So why did Makó become famous for its onions? The town had two secrets. One was that of growing onions in biennial cycles. The first year the growers cultivated only seed onions. What is more, before replanting the results, they dried them in winter above their stoves, thus ensuring a quality crop. The following August, the fields of Makó were overflowing with fist-size, shiny-skinned, zesty onions with high vitamin and sugar content. In addition to these attributes, onions grown this way could easily be stored and shipped; and, indeed, they found their way to distant places, including Western Europe.

These days, sellers at Hungarian food markets who seek to inspire confidence in shoppers often advertise their onions by placing a little sign in front of them with the words *makói hagyma* (onions from Makó). Of course, if you happen to be shopping in such a market and notice that the said onions are prepackaged, don't be ashamed about taking a closer look to see where in fact they grew—for nowadays Hungary gets some "Makó" onions from as far away as China.

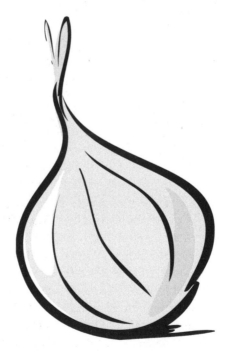

# drinks

## Jolán Mann

When Hungarians were asked in a public opinion survey in the recent past to name the alcoholic drinks they consider to be the most quintessentially Hungarian, wine came first (74.2%), *pálinka* second (14.9%), and beer third (7.7%).

Hungarians have been known for centuries even abroad as a nation of wine drinkers. The country's rich vinicultural heritage was made possible by climactic conditions; a moderately dry summer followed by a long, sunny Indian summer; various regional microclimates; and the geological configuration of wine regions.

Hungarian wine began making a name for itself in other parts of Europe beginning at the turn of the sixteenth century. As early as the fifteenth century, physicians held the sweet aszú wine of Tokaj to have curative properties, and indeed *Vinum tokajense passum* was sold in apothecaries. The Latin saying *"vinum regum, rex vinorum"* (wine of kings, king of wines) derived from the fact that Tokaj Aszú, especially in the eighteenth century, became a favorite wine of European rulers, some of whom just couldn't live without it, as evidenced by yet another saying: *"Non est vinum, nisi tokainum"—There is no other wine, only Tokaj.*

Aszú grapes are the product of a fungi that engenders a noble rot, which makes its way into grapes under favorable climactic conditions. Tokaj wine was made famous by these aszú grapes; more specifically, by both dry and sweet *szamorodni* wine made with a mix of these grapes and the must of healthy grapes—but especially by the noble, sweet aszú wines. The value of these prized Tokay Aszú wines (graded from a low of 3 to a high of 6) increases in proportion with the number of *puttonyok* of grapes used in its making—a *puttony* being what in viniculture is referred to in English as a "butt" (i.e., a cask), its capacity being 42–46 kilograms. Another key factor is the number of years the wine has had to mature, which is always at least two more than the puttony number on the label.

Hungary has six wine regions and, within these, twenty-two wine districts. Southeastern Hungary's Danube region is both the largest and youngest, producing light, crisp, fruity wines, and the Kunság is its most important district. The Southern Pannónia and the Northern Pannonia regions west of the Danube are, meanwhile, known for their variety of wines. The former, in southcentral Hungary, includes the Villány-Siklós and the Szekszárd districts; and the latter, in northwestern Hungary, is home to the Sopron, the Mór, and the Ászár-Neszmély districts.

The nation's most variegated wine region is the one around Lake Balaton, famous chiefly for its white wines. Its constituent districts include, most prominently, Badacsony, Balatonfüred-Csopak, Balatonfelvidék, and Somló.

The prolific Hungarian writer Béla Hamvas (1897–1968) declared in his book-length essay, *A bor filozófiája* (The Philosophy of Wine), that Somló wine is Hungary's only "universal" wine—by which he meant that it is one of the world's few wines that all of humanity could drink simultaneously on one big holiday. Somló wine is also called "the wedding night wine," since popular belief has it that it helps along the conception of a male child. Is it surprising, then, that the male scions of the House of Habsburg had to fill up on Somló wine in the run-up to their wedding nights?

Most prominent among the various wines of northern Hungary's Eger wine district, within the wine region of the same name, is *bikavér* (Bull's Blood)—a dry, noble red wine produced from at least three types of grapes. Alongside Tokaj Aszú, Bull's Blood is Hungary's second flagship wine. It is also made in Szekszárd.

Since 2002, the Tokaj-Hegyalja wine region—a UNESCO World Heritage area that comprises twenty-seven communities and 7,000 hectares (17, 300 acres) of vineyards—is Hungary's only wine region or district that produces wine whose label indicates its exact origin.

Ever since the turn of the twentieth century, Hungarians have been fond of mixing wine with seltzer. The credit goes in no small part to scientist *Ányos Jedlik* (1800–95), who devised a simpler and more economical method of manufacturing carbonated water.

The Hungarian language shows its inventiveness in naming no less than four types of *fröccs* (wine-and-soda) typically ordered in bars. These differ in their relative proportions of wine and seltzer (one deciliter, or roughly a cup, being the standard measure). There is the *kisfröccs* (little fröccs), which consists of an equal amount of wine and seltzer (1 dl each) and its big brother, the *nagyfröccs* (big fröccs) (2 dl wine, 1 dl seltzer). A more diluted alternative is the *hosszú-lépés* (long step), which contains 1 dl of wine and 2 dl of seltzer. But, if we're really thirsty, we can ask for a *házmester*, whose even more colorful, if somewhat enigmatic, name means *concierge* in English: this boasts 3 dl of wine and 2 dl of seltzer. And then there is the *házmester*'s opposite, proportion-wise: the *viceházmester* (assistant concierge), with 2 dl wine and 3 dl seltzer.

Mihály Zichy (1827–1906), *A bor hatalma* (The Power of Wine)

If we're even more averse to overdoing it on the alcohol, we might settle for any of Hungary's various exceptionally tasty brands of mineral water, with which we can likewise quench our thirst. Some such wondrous waters, which typically come from deep underground, are indeed so packed with a particular composition of minerals that they are commonly called *gyógyvíz* (curative water) and are considered effective at treating various ailments.

True *pálinka*, which comprises 100 percent fruit distillate, is the second most "Hungarian" alcoholic drink. The word *pálinka*, which is of Slovak origin and enjoys European Union protection, replaced the earlier, Hungarian term *égettbor* (literally: burnt wine). Traditionally, country folk made their own *pálinka* in relatively elaborate private distilleries in a practice called *kisüsti-főzés*, which thrived unfettered until its prohibition in 1920. However, the adjective *kisüsti* is still sometimes used today when referring to high quality, homemade *pálinka*.

Celebrated regional varieties of *pálinka* and centers of *pálinka* production arose from the private distilleries of the *kisüsti* era; for example, the peach *pálinka* of Göncz and Kecskemét, and the plum *pálinka* of Szatmár (i.e., of the Szatmár region, after a historic administrative county of the Kingdom of Hungary that in the present-day comprises northwest Hungary and northeast Romania).

The oldest types of Hungarian *pálinka* derive from wine and by-products of wine-making. The core ingredient of *törkölypálinka* (marc brandy), for example, is the *törköly* (marc), which consists of the plant matter that remains behind after grapes are pressed (e.g., tendrils, skin, and seeds).

The most celebrated of Hungarian fruit brandies is Kecskemét's *fütyülős barackpálinka* (literally: whistling peach brandy). It is easily recognizable on account of its long-necked bottle, which can supposedly be used to whistle. In all of Hungary's neighbors, the favorite raw material for distilling fruit brandy are plums—

which produces what the Slavs call *slivovitz* and Hungarians call *szilvapálinka* (plum *pálinka*); in Hungary, the best such pálinka is made in the country's eastern half, in Szabolcs-Szatmár and Békés counties. Among the flavored fruit brandies traditionally made in the homes of country folk is *ágyaspálinka*. Today also mass-produced in modern facilities, *ágyaspálinka* contains spices, herbs, fruit, and or seeds that are added right to the bottle, yielding a zesty spirit whose name means literally "bedded *pálinka*," as its extra, flavor-packed ingredients are, in effect, bedded into the bottle. It features a wide-ranging alcohol content, from 30% to 50%.

Hungary's most famous spiced liquor is a reputedly therapeutic herbal bitter concocted by one Dr. Zwack back in the nineteenth century. This has been manufactured since 1883 under the name *Unicum* in unmistakably dark, short-necked, round bottles that are ubiquitous in Hungarian supermarkets and liquor stores to this day.

Although brewing and beer drinking goes way back in Hungary—indeed, beer was known even in the court of King Matthias—the increasing ubiquity of wine and *pálinka* saw beer eventually fall into third place on Hungarians' list of "most Hungarian" alcoholic drinks. Beer's waning prestige in Hungary over the centuries was probably also due to the fact that in the modern age, Hungarian national identity was formed in part by a conscious tendency to eschew German identity; and, of course, beer was and is much beloved by peoples of Germanic stock. Indeed, the fate of beer-drinking customs in Hungary even came to reflect the nation's aspirations for independence. Legend has it that the Austrian executioners of the thirteen Hungarian generals put to death in the town of Arad at the tragic close of Hungary's 1848–49 revolution clinked their beer mugs to celebrate the occasion. And so the nationality-conscious Hungarians, even if they could not quite bring themselves to desist with beer drinking altogether, did manage to avoid clinking glasses or mugs (as the case may be) for 150 years. Although the validity of this resolution expired a few years back, many a Hungarian beer drinker of the twenty-first century sticks to it even today.

# entertainment

## Adrienn Szentesi

In Budapest, there are many places and many forms of entertainment. These include distinguished and popular theaters, Europe's second largest chain of art film cinemas (after Paris), exhibit galleries, concert halls, museums, cultural festivals, restaurants, taverns, open-air entertainment venues; and places to kick back and relax, drink in hand, in the crumbling inner courtyards of decaying old apartment buildings. Yes, all this and more can be found in Hungary's capital. Allow me to pick out of this embarrassment of riches two annual events, both of which have grown into huge institutions in recent years; so huge, in fact, that today each of them has a well-established international reputation and, indeed, draws throngs of visitors from abroad. These are the Tavaszi Fesztivál (Spring Festival) and the Sziget Fesztivál (*sziget* meaning *island*, but known as *Sziget Festival* even in English). One offers top-notch high culture; the other, the best of pop culture. As opposites, they draw two different types of audiences. Still, they can be neither compared nor contrasted. Each has carved out for itself an enduring reputation, one that has already written itself into Hungary's—and Europe's—entertainment history books.

The Budapest Spring Festival dates back to 1981. The tradition and, simultaneously, the mission of this event is twofold: presenting to the world the cream of the crop of Hungarian culture, and introducing Hungarian audiences to the international arts. The program features primarily classical music orchestral concerts and chamber recitals, opera and ballet performances, theatrical productions by distinguished drama companies, folk music and dance performances, jazz concerts, and art exhibits. Participating institutions invariably

162    

include the Hungarian State Concert Orchestra, the Budapest Festival
Orchestra, and the National Philharmonic.

In the first phase of the Spring Festival's existence, from 1981–90, the
festival was owned and operated by the National Tourism Office. The
program during this period included attractions such as an exhibit by
the sculptor Amerigo Tot (1982); a piano recital by Keith Jarrett (1985);
a performance by the Győr Ballet under director Iván Markó (1986);
the Franz Liszt Chamber Orchestra with André Maurice (1988); and
an aria evening with Monserrat Caballé (1990).

From 1991–96 the Spring Festival was under the management of
the Interart Festival Center, and it was expanded from ten days to
three weeks. On the menu during this period: a melody- and aria
evening with José Carreras (1992), Chinese opera (1993); an exhibit
of paintings by Tivadar Csontvary-Kosztka (1994); and the Martha
Graham Dance Company (1996).

In 1997 the festival was taken over by a nonprofit company, the
Budapest Fesztiválközpont (Budapest Festival Center), under the
direction of Zsófia Zimányi. Among the most memorable programs in
the years since: the London Philharmonic Orchestra (1999), Moscow's
Taganka Theater (2001), "Astor Piazzolla Nights" featuring the tango
tunes of the late, great composer by this name (2004); and Zubin
Mehta with Florence's Maggio Musicale orchestra (2005).

The Budapest Spring Festival (www.btf.hu) occupies an illustrious
place indeed among Europe's numerous cultural celebrations of
international prominence.

*Sziget Festival.* Appropriately enough, this grand event transpires
in August of each year on the northern reaches of Óbudai sziget
(Óbuda Island), well outside downtown in the Óbuda district of
northern Budapest.

Here's the Sziget experience, in a nutshell: Let's say you're hankering
for a week of togetherness, for that communal feeling. Seven full
days. Wednesday to Wednesday. To the max. Then you collapse. Four
p.m. You're on Batthány Square, right across the Danube from the
Parliament Building. There, you head underground, buy a ticket for

the HÉV—the commuter train, that is—and squeeze aboard. You go about a half dozen stops (who's counting?) and get off at *Filatori-gát*. A million people—sure feels like it, anyway. Heat. Sweat. Waiting by the entrance for half an hour. You walk across the bridge. Across the Danube. A restrained rumble, a muffled boom. The music grows ever louder. It comes from here, there, and everywhere. You're look for a site, pitch a tent. Happy faces all around. Young people looking for a good time. Dust. Your mouth, lungs, nose are full of it. A program. Hmm. Where shall we go? Where to meet? Drifting from one stage to another. Here and there you stop, talk, stay a while. Your planned schedule is all washed up. Friends old and new, unfamiliar acquaintances. The place "brings us together." Everyone, everywhere. Time to telephone. Text messages on your mobile. Drinking. Eating. Gals and guys. Flirting with the femmes, having fun with the fellows. The crowd is bigger by the minute. By the second. You're running about. Where are your friends? What the hell. You'll lose track of them, anyway. From concert to concert you go. Ear-popping decibels, dancing till you drop. It doesn't matter who you are and where you're going. All that matters here is the music, the dancing, the togetherness. In peace and love. Techno fans and hard-core fans living it up side by side. Gasping for air. Yet another waterfall of alcohol rushes down your throat. Another stroll, another concert. Two a.m. By now you're just dragging your tired feet, but you peek into this and that tent. You try tracking down your friends. Four a.m. Where the hell did I pitch my tent? All at once, you see it! Dirty and exhausted, but transformed, you flop down on your mattress. Morning comes. Time to stand in line for a shower. Ice-cold water strikes your numb back. Never again. Never again a morning like this. But by afternoon it all begins again. You don't leave out a single day. You can't. The Sziget has you in its grip. Every fiber of your being. A week later, you're pouting away over the fact that the next Sziget is a whole year off.

The Sziget Festival dates back to the wee hours of one fine morning in 1993, when musician Péter "Sziámi" Müller and concert organizer Károly Gerendai were on their way home on their band's bus. They were dreaming away. About one really big music festival. The dogged determination of eight or ten people soon paid off. The Sziget Festival got rolling August 19, 1993, with 200 concerts, 80 films, 40 plays, 10,000 tent sites, a day pass for 300 forints (around $1.50), a weekly pass for 1,800 forints ($9), and 60,000 people. Only Hungarian bands, a small budget, and a loss of 3.5 million forints ($15,000). The turning point came in 1997. That's when the Sziget became an international event with the works—huge infrastructure, stars from abroad, serious sponsors. By 2005 this annual, week-long festival could boast a record 385,000 visitors; 170 foreign bands and performers, 450 Hungarian ones; a day pass for 5,000 forints ($25), and a weekly pass between 20,000 and 30,000 forints ($100–$150), depending on whether you bought one early or waited until the last minute; and, yes, a profit in the tens of millions (of forints, true—but it still sounds good).

The Sziget Festival (www.sziget.hu/festival/english) has become Europe's largest, best music festival of all.

Last but not least, today we Hungarians have ample opportunities for quality entertainment even well outside of Budapest. The first years of the twenty-first century saw a burgeoning of summer festivals, especially those devoted to music. To name but a few: Early July sees the Volt Fesztivál (www.sziget.hu/volt/english) in the lovely western city of Sopron (contemporary rock, jazz, and electronica). Mid-July brings Balaton Sound (www.sziget.hu/balatonsound_english), geared mainly toward electronica fans, but whose chief attraction is really that the partying unfolds on the shore of Lake Balaton, in the cool beach town of Zamárdi. The Hegyalja Fesztivál (www.hegyaljafestival. hu), in the legendary wine village of Tokaj, in northwest Hungary, is yet another highlight of July. And early August takes us back to Lake Balaton—more specifically, to villages flanking the hills just north of Lake Balaton, which play host to the Művészetek Völgye (Valley of the Arts; www.muveszetekvolgye.hu—Hungarian only), a grand festival that brings together jazz, folk music, and world music, as well as visual and other arts.

# sport

## Gábor Vaderna

On August 24, 2008, the world watched as three of the players on Hungary's Olympic water polo team tried pushing their coach, Dénes Kemény, into a pool in Beijing. Rather than wait for the inevitable, Kemény obligingly leapt in. His clothes were sopping wet, but he clearly couldn't care less. Only a minute earlier, his team had defeated the United States to defend the golds it won in the two—yes, two—previous Olympics. It's always happiness itself to win an Olympic medal, but perhaps it is all the more so to defend an Olympic championship.

In Hungary, the national water polo team, which Kemény heads, also goes by the name Gold Team. With mostly the same lineup they have won three Olympic golds; one gold and four silver medals at world championships; and two golds, four silvers, and three bronze medals at European championships. Theirs is the world's best water polo team. Wherever they have appeared, they have been the favorites, and more often than not they have come away as victors. That day at the 2008 Beijing Olympics was not the first occasion that the players, all caught up in the moment, had thrown Coach Kemény into the pool.

Hungarians like being in water. When it comes to aquatic sports, we expect medals, whatever the international competition. Swimming, water polo, kayaking, and canoeing. Women's, men's. It matters not a bit. In this realm we've always had our share of international stars. It's as if the grand past, the splendor of bygone championships, always gives strength for newer triumphs. We're talking tradition here. One generation passes down its knowledge to the next.

Even literally so. Dénes Kemény's father likewise played water polo and then began coaching, like his son. This was not the first time that onetime legendary water polo players went on to become legendary coaches; an athletic career does not come to an end once one is no longer young. Perhaps this, too, goes to explain why Hungary's national water polo teams have been the most successful of all time. They have reaped eight golds, three silvers, and three bronze medals at the Olympics; two golds, five silvers, and two bronze medals at world championships; and no less than twelve golds, four silvers, and three bronze medals at European championships. Between 1928 and 1980 the team came away with a medal at every single Olympics. They've gotten so many golds that a silver here, a bronze there, counts practically as a failure.

Good traditions are not enough, of course; a good team is also essential. And, indeed, the Hungarian team is always just that. It's a good team even when it defends its Olympic gold with its star veterans, as did the team in 2004; and as was the case with the other Gold Team back in the 1950s. It's a good team even when it debuts with a whole new lineup, as when it defended its first-place position at an Olympics in the 1930s. And the team can safely be called good also when it happens not to defend a gold it won at the previous Olympics, but simply to capture a new one after a hiatus.

Of course, all this might be too little, too. It's also essential that the players stay calm at that all-important moment, and that the coaches embark on championships with a winning strategy. The Hungarian team has been good even when the same players were constantly playing in matches, as at the 1976 Montreal Olympics; and likewise when a different lineup jumped into the pool at almost every match—for example, at the 1952 Helsinki Olympics. It's been good when the gold has been decided in the course of team matches, and also in knock-out competitions. This is not to mention those cases where they had to improve their goal difference and where it was enough to win by a single goal.

But all this might be too little, too. Good conditions are a must.

Before the 1932 Olympics, the Hungarian team that would go on to take the gold performed at gala matches in order to cover its travel expenses. Hungary today lays claim to one of the world's strongest water polo championships, and perhaps the best system for coaching the water polo teams of the future.

Does this cost a lot of money? Not so much. Resolve and perseverance are more important: the conviction that the sport itself, and the joy of participating in it, is more important than anything and everything. This is why Hungarian water polo has always proved capable of coming back. If, after years brimming with success, three Olympics pass by without a medal—it's as if this hasn't happened. The team will next come home with two in a row. There is no setback after which Hungarian water polo isn't capable of coming back, ready to take on the world anew.

And, of course, it comes back not only because Dénes Kemény likes being thrown into the pool—though there might be something to that, too.

# woman

## Péter Rácz

After a visit to Budapest in the late 1950s, the popular French cabaret singer and actor (and ladies man) Yves Montand remarked, "The most beautiful woman I have ever seen in my life was a Hungarian." Think what we may of Yves Montand, we can neither ignore this assessment nor deny it. The matter at hand, I must emphasize, need neither be womanly beauty nor for that matter need it be beautiful women. We (men) would rightly be accused of heavy-handedness (or, better put: heavy-mindedness) if women inspired in us only thoughts of beauty; which is to say, if we didn't ponder the question of why, when pondering (womanly) beauty, we should automatically associate it with other virtues. Moral virtues, moreover!

Indeed, certain women inspire us men to musings that seem light years from "beauty." It was in Hungary, for example, that one fine day I happened across a woman who struck me as the homeliest imaginable. Did my thoughts of her stop there? Far from it. It so happened that I was to be in her company for a week, and the opportunity to devote this week to studying just what it was that had rendered her countenance so unappealing so consumed me that, in the end, she captured a bit of my heart! She was from Ireland, by the way, but that's beside the point. She might just as well have been Hungarian, too.

So then, the Hungarian woman is . . . No, a sentence can't begin like this! One woman is like this, after all, and another is like that. If one woman is fiery, whether in body or mind or both, sure enough there's another woman out there who is sleepy and sluggish and lumpish and unimaginative—and indeed her presence serves to counterbalance the effect upon us men of those wondrous women who sweep us away with their dazzling exteriors and interiors, their intellectual vigor, and their radiating instincts. Hungarian women are just the beings that (Hungarian) men want to see, that they notice, and that they respect.

Are Hungarian women accommodating, or do they expect others to be so? Are they seductive, obliging, erotic, domineering, or slavish? Are they high-strung and hustled and bustled only to then outlive their husbands by twenty years in a second flowering? Are they as visual artists see them, as poets and writers write about them? If they're not only like this, who is there to paint a better, fuller picture of them? Social historians? Or they themselves?

Does the fact that a women's movement has yet to get off the ground in Hungary since the outset of democracy in 1990 mean that most Magyar women don't feel a pressing need to create one, that some have hit formidable roadblocks in their efforts to do so—or both? That there are not only men, but also women, who excel at painting and writing is naturally no more a new phenomenon in Hungary than it is in so many other reaches of the globe. But what is to come of the fact that those Hungarian women who have tried breaking ground by studying the achievements of women in particular have been largely unsuccessful in watering the seedling of "gender studies" into life in higher education? To date, this seedling is hardly viable; it is encircled by a whole army of indifferent men. And yet there are women worthy of respect who deal with women's literature; and, indeed, there are women worthy of even greater respect who give birth to literature—that is, literature whose most salient attributes are aesthetic rather than gender-specific ones.

Incidentally, does literature by men about women (among other themes) portray women's social role, capture a model of behavior, shape thought, or all of the above? If so, why should it?

And what are we to make of the fact that Hungarian women— who no longer sit on tractors, as so many of them did more than fifty years ago, but who today work across broad sectors of society and have indeed completely womanized certain trades—have yet to switch saddles, so to speak, and occupy professions of high social standing in substantial numbers?

Why is it that Hungarian women gladly read poems about themselves—about women—but, judging from those who get published, at any rate, don't write similar poems about men? Are men inclined to write poems about women so as to avoid having to admit what wonderful stuff is written about women by women? Does all this stem from an underlying conviction that the alfa and omega of every being is woman—but that the crown of creation is man? Or vice versa?

Will a Hungarian amazon be born who will resolve to transform our image of women by creating a whole new category of literary works? By sweeping off the nation's literary palate those classic lines of love poetry that just happen to be by men—by such time-honored literary figures as Bálint Balassi, Endre Ady, Árpád Tóth, Dezső Kosztolányi, Attila József, and György Petri? Or will a literary woman be born who will at least pose questions as farcical as did the great humorist writer Frigyes Karinthy (1887–1938), when he asked: who kisses more, men or women?

Until some or all of this comes to pass to substantially reshape popular stereotypes, we should not be too surprised that the mass media continues to highlight this sort of news about Hungarian women, which hit the papers in July 2005:

*According to media pundits, a new TV star has been born in Italy. The Hungarian-born former hard porn star Éva Henger attracts six million viewers nightly to her entertainment program. And, with this, she further reinforces Italians' conviction that it is not by chance that Hungarian women reign supreme over Italian porn, that Hungarian women see the most success in Italian nightclubs, and that Budapest is the capital of porn.*

It seems the Italians know: everything—and that includes every woman—is beautiful if we look long enough. That said, as Bob Marley sang it: *no woman, no cry.*

# man

## Noémi Kiss

Men are the pillar of Hungarian society. You can lean on them. Even today, when in so many European countries women enjoy equal opportunities, in Hungary, men are the dominant presence in the steering of society, in the formulating of political opinions, in science, in the media, and so on. Just why is this so? Because Hungarian men are so extraordinary? This is true and, well, it's also *not* true.

The Hungarian man, when he's still young, is dashing, persuasive, and inventive. He embarks on life brimming with talent, he dresses well, he excels at sports, and he is a passionate suitor. The Hungarian man proves his love in every area of life. For the world's most beautiful woman he faces death if need be. Even today there are men in Hungary who bring a flower on a first date, assuming they want to win a woman's heart. Indeed, we can even encounter young Magyar men in this day and age who write poems to their loves, just like the great Renaissance poet Bálint Balassi. True, over the course of his life the Hungarian man wins the hearts of many women, but if he says he loves us, we needn't always believe him. For example, György Petri, one of Hungary's best known bards of the second half of the twentieth century, once wrote in a poem, five hundred years after Bálint Balassi, that over the course of his life he was

Mihály Zichy (1827–1906),
*Hegytetőn* (On the Mountaintop)

involved with 150 women—and presumably he loved each one, in his own way. Hungarian men have therefore changed a lot over time. So why shouldn't it be advisable to trust in the fidelity of the Hungarian man? After all, Magyar males have vowed fidelity in some of the world's loveliest poems! It is not by chance that, among ethnic Hungarians in neighboring Transylvania, the dandelion is known by the name *Férfihűség* (Male Fidelity).

Whether on Lake Balaton or elsewhere on a summertime beach in Hungary—where water is a key accessory of warm-weather adventures—we can readily observe the changes in the male body. We can witness the Magyar man grow older, develop a beer belly, and move a whole lot less than back in his dating days. By the same token, other males turn positively beefy and hang a gold chain around their necks. Some, we notice, are busy reading a book or a newspaper, or else are out sailing or playing tennis. But in vain. Most Magyar males love beer, and it shows. The transformation begins in their twenties, when they get married. In most Hungarian families there is a traditional division of labor. The wife does the laundry, cooks, cleans, and raises the children, while the man officially earns money. By night, of course, he drinks beer.

According to some studies, Magyar males are among the most susceptible men in the world to midlife-crisis–related depression and suicidal tendencies. The most typical and, of course, dramatic male malady is the heart attack, which ensues from lots of stress and from the rigors and uncertainties of earning a living. And so the Hungarian man is often down in the dumps. Consequently he is given to giving up on love, and from an early age he yearns for something entirely different from what he was born into. True, he doesn't share such sentiments with anyone, because the Hungarian man is expected to come across as strong and well balanced. Magyar males are, however, sensitive and chock full of wit; they follow the world's every oscillation, and most Hungarian women stand by their partners to the end of their lives.

The Hungarian man's greatest virtue is manliness. With few

exceptions, Magyar mothers today still raise their sons on this principle. Ever since the nineteenth century, manliness in Hungary has indeed meant a strict set of principles. It obliges the Hungarian man to exhibit a noble bearing, mature thinking, and levelheadedness. Sober political judgments. The Hungarian man is virtuous so long as he is ever on the move, he spurns death, he flouts pain, he never sheds a tear, and indeed he deliberately seeks out danger.

All these virtues are bundled up in the figure of Toldi, that literary character who represented the male ideal of Hungarian Romanticism. Set to verse by the great nineteenth-century poet János Arany, Toldi is a man of great strength. But this is not enough to make him happy. He needs a woman to soften his soul, to soothe him, and if need be, to follow him everywhere; while of course she, the woman, represses any propensity she may harbor to realize her own potential.

Today, Hungarian women are beginning to view manliness in starkly different terms. More than a few recently established women's organizations and magazines are protesting vociferously against one-time male virtues and privileges and against the patriarchal family. In their assessment, it would be all for the better if Hungarian men could free themselves of the burden of tradition and adopt a more flexible view of manliness, allowing women more opportunity to realize their own potential. That is, the members of each gender could be free to decide how they conceive of the ideal (Hungarian) man. That said, most Hungarian women desire nothing more than to be seduced by a real Hungarian man.

# businessman

## István Bori

Once upon a time, on the far side of the Alps but on the near side of
the Carpathians, there was a Hungary. It happened to be making war
just then, but little sense did all this make to *Sanyika* ("little Sándor,"
that is, Sándor being his given name), who was born in 1943 in a
small Transylvanian village, Börvely. His dad had perished in the war,
and so he and his two little sisters were fatherless from an early age.

That evil sorcerer, Fate, had in store a hard childhood for *Sanyika*.
In 1944 the three children and their mother had to leave their village.
They moved hundreds of kilometers westward all the way to Etyek,
beside the kingdom's largest city, Budapest. The mother was compelled
to place her children in an orphanage for a little while. Every day
was a challenge for *Sanyika*, for instead of going to school he had to
walk several kilometers every single weekday to a well to fetch water.
However, the well-meaning gentleman who was his teacher always
made up for the missed lessons, and he bestowed *Sanyika* with a love
of books. As he sprouted into a young man, *Sándor* (which he was
now being called much more often than as a little boy) picked himself
up by the bootstraps. By the age of ten he kept rabbits, and he was
doing brisk business with a toy so dear to him—leather footballs.
"Why, he'll wind up becoming a merchant," folks around him said
disapprovingly—and, indeed, that's just what he became. A merchant.
After finishing college, Sándor went off into the world to try his luck.
Three trials awaited him.

At first he found work in the Fejér County branch of the (state-
sanctioned and state-owned) company ÁFÉSZ, an acronym for the
Hungarian words "General Consumers' and Sales Cooperative."

There he had to take on the seven-headed dragon of bureaucracy, which didn't take kindly to *Comrade Sándor's* pushing at the bounds of socialism. He established industrial facilities, and indeed he was even jailed for a short time as a result. However, *Comrade Sándor* didn't give in, and of course he always had protectors who saved him from the claws of the seven-head dragon.

The second trial was even harder. Beyond the Glass Mountain, at the edge of the Western world, in Vienna, Sándor happened upon the Stafa department store, which took hold of his imagination and just wouldn't let go. On getting home to Hungary he finagled his way around bureaucracy until, in 1973, he established the era's most successful chain of department stores, SKÁLA—the first such stores in communist-era Hungary where you could pick things off the shelf or clothes rack directly without having to ask some glum-faced clerk behind a counter to get something for you. SKÁLA became ubiquitous; it became an icon. Quite possibly there was no one in Hungary who did not know of it. Whether it sold low-cost tomatoes or rugs, there was a time when the seven-headed dragon of bureaucracy—who knows why—did not take kindly to it all.

These were beautiful but trying times, which Hungarians remember most of all—as regards SKÁLA, that is—for the chain's main advertising gimmick: a stick figure of a boy we knew endearingly as SKÁLA's Little Rascal, who proclaimed while dancing about on TV, "I am SKÁLA Co-op's Little Rascal." (There's a pun wrapped up in all this that further explains why it is so memorable to Hungarians; namely, the word for "Little Rascal" in Hungarian is *kopé*, and it just so happens that "SKÁLA Co-op's" is "*SKÁLA Co-op-é*"; hence *kopé* equals *Co-op-é*. Get it? Never mind. Read on.)

But the real "rascal" was *Sándor* himself, who, while further forcing the bounds of de facto socialism, gathered a little army of like-minded folks around him with whom the third trial no longer seemed impossible.

This trial occurred in 1986. *Comrade Sándor* cobbled together a bank. This became Magyar Hitelbank (Hungarian Credit Bank). By then, the seven-headed dragon of bureaucracy had tamed somewhat, and *Sándor*, sensing that Hungary was in for big changes sooner rather than later, participated actively in the process of "capitalization." As a bank director he played puppet man in the "birth" of virtually all of Hungary's billionaire entrepreneurs. (Note that the "billions" at issue here are in Hungarian forints, which admittedly add up to much less than a billion dollars; but even a billion forints is nothing to sneeze at.) He passed the third trial, and meanwhile Hungary's political system underwent a sea change as "state socialism" (aka communism) collapsed. *President and Managing Director Sándor* finally found himself where he'd always wanted to fit in—on the international market, where competition is king, and where being a "little rascal" is par for the course.

He yearned for an international career, and his Hungarian-American friends across the great big ocean gave him the start-up capital to do so. He made his first million (and now we're talking dollars) in Russia—capitalizing on the lessons he'd learned during socialism—and then he embarked on huge real-estate ventures. His company, TriGránit (note the word granite in the name), built such glittery temples of consumption in Budapest as the Pólus Center and West End City Center shopping malls. Today *Mr. Sándor*'s name is known far and wide not only in Hungary but in the whole region. In 2007 he opened a huge movie studio, Korda Studios, in his onetime village of Etyek. His business ventures are generally predestined to success, with one exception: not even he managed to revive his favorite onetime sport, Hungarian soccer, from the ashes of death as regards its international prospects. There, not even being a little rascal helped.

This little entrepreneurial fairytale was about Sándor Demján, whose career is simultaneously typical and anomalous as far as Hungarian capitalists are concerned. As everywhere in the world, the Hungarian businessman comes in different stripes and sizes: wealthy and successful or failed and dirt poor; an entrepreneur out of necessity or else the founder of a business empire; isolated from and suspicious of the world, or else sensitive to social issues. Doing "business" became a legitimate activity in Hungary with the fall of communism, but no sooner did this happen than it was also enveloped by mystique: getting rich quick, legendary financial transactions and privatizations, skyrocketing careers, and of course, underworld connections that cast a shadow over all of this. In 1990s Hungary, the "entrepreneur" appeared in the public mind above all as a convicted criminal, or, worse, as a corpse on a cobblestone street.

This negative image of entrepreneurs associated with Hungary's free-reined capitalism has made a deep mark in the public mind. Nor does the continuing tendency of the nation's economic elite to ensconce themselves from society-at-large hold promise that this stereotype might fade anytime soon. To the average person, the visible and invisible walls that surround them suggest a "fairytale world." True, this is a world that has a bit of catching up to do before it joins the ranks of the international jet set: the wealthiest Hungarian entrepreneurs typically boast net worths only to a humble hundreds of millions of dollars. One notable exception is, of course, Sándor Demján, who comfortably exceeded the one billion dollar mark by 2007. As for those people of Hungarian descent who earned their millions or billions in America or Canada, such as Peter Munk and George Soros, and who rank among the world's most influential businessmen, they comprise a different kettle of rich fish.

# athlete

## Gábor Vaderna

Ferenc Puskás or, as he is endearingly called in Hungary, Puskás Öcsi (Puskás the Lad), was a soccer player. The most celebrated Hungarian soccer player of all time. And perhaps the most celebrated Hungarian abroad. Wherever we go in the world where soccer is loved and watched—and soccer is, after all, loved and watched most everywhere in the world—people know the name Puskás. He was the most successful inside left of all time, the best goal-kicker of all time, one of the greatest all-around players of all time, a world-class player for Hungary's Gold Team, and a player on no less than two national teams.

What more can we say about Puskás, after all? Let's let the numbers speak first.

Puskás played on a Hungarian national championship–winning team no less than five times and was the country's top scorer four times. Between 1942 and 1956 he kicked 358 goals in 249 Hungarian championship matches. He won six Spanish league titles, the Spanish cup (Copa del Rey) twice, was top scorer in Spain five times, scored 324 goals for Real Madrid in 372 official matches, won three European Champion Clubs' Cup titles (1958-59, 1959-60, and 1965-66), was twice runner-up in the European Cup (1961-62, 1963-64), was top scorer in the European Cup series twice, scored thirty-four goals in thirty-nine European Cup matches for Real Madrid, and was top scorer once in at the Intercontinental Cup. In 1952 he was a member of the Hungarian team that triumphed at the Olympic Games, in 1953 he was top scorer at the European Cup, in 1954 he was a member of the Hungarian silver-medal–winning World Cup team; and in 1962, when playing for the Spanish national team, he reached twelfth place at the World Cup. Between 1945 and 1956 he was capped no less than eighty-four times by Hungary and scored eighty-three goals for his country, a record that has gone unsurpassed since; and in the early 1960s he was capped four times by Spain.

And what was necessary to achieve all this? Simple. One right foot and one left foot. But, still, Puskás was better than anyone else, particularly with his left foot. Explosiveness, exquisite handling of the ball, inscrutable technique, a wealth of ideas, all-round sparkling soccer. A true playmaker, one who not only scored great goals but also a player whose geometrically precise long balls allowed his fellow players to excel. Which was his best goal? Hard to say. He scored so many great goals, after all. At the 1952 Olympics, in a semifinal match against the Swedes, he scored a goal from eighteen meters (almost fifty-nine feet) away from an acute angle with the outside of his left foot, so that the ball hit the left post before ending up in the back of the net—an unexpected shot that few players could equal, executed perfectly by Puskás. On November 25, 1953, he scored what may have been his most famous goal at what the British press proclaimed "the game of the century"—a match in London between the Hungarian and the English national teams that the Magyars won 6-3, marking the first time the English had ever lost such a game at home. After a brilliant attack, Puskás tricked Wright, the English goalkeeper, by pulling the ball back, then delivered a shot at medium height with his left foot that sailed into the net. Puskás is featured in practically every documentary film ever made on the heyday of soccer. But that's enough listing of his goals; for they simply must be seen, not just read about.

Puskás first played in a Hungarian national premier league at age sixteen, and on his debut for the national team at age eighteen he introduced himself, as it were, by scoring a goal. He kicked a goal at the legendary 6-3 match in the final of the 1952 Olympic Games, and in 1954 at the World Cup final that Hungary lost. Puskás found the net in nearly every game he ever played. In the 1950s in

Hungary, he played for the world's best club (Kispest-Honvéd) and best national team (the so-called Golden Team), and after defecting from Hungary in 1956, he again found himself on the world's best club team, Real Madrid. He went from being the communist dictatorship's preeminent athlete and the very embodiment of national pride to being a traitor who had fled the country, only to ultimately return as a hero to his native land.

Hungary's defeat at the 1954 World Cup was a real national trauma, and to this day some people excel at coming up with excuses for what happened. What's certain, though, is that afterward, the communist regime was not so inclined to forgive the country's star players for every little misstep. Up until then, Puskás had consciously played the part of celebrity just as much in everyday life as on the field—no small accomplishment in the harsh dictatorship of 1950s Hungary. But after that unforgettable match in Bern in 1954, not even he could get away with everything; which is why, on one occasion, in a May 1956 match against Czechoslovakia, he was barred from playing, ostensibly because he was out of shape. (Indeed, the Hungarian national team lost 4-2.) At the time of the 1956 revolution, the  bad boy of Hungarian soccer took part along with other top Hungarian players in a soccer tour of South America even though they didn't have official permission to do so. Some of the world-class Kispest-Honvéd players on the tour—for example, Puskás's childhood friend József Bozsik and the legendary goalkeeper of the national team, Gyula Grosics—returned to Hungary, but the three Hungarian strikers (Puskás, Sándor Kocsis, and Zoltán Czibor) decided that if they went back home they'd be in for hefty punishment. Ultimately, all three ended up in Spain, two of them on Barcelona's team and Puskás with Real Madrid. In the Spanish capital the aging, twenty-nine year old player with an all-too conspicuous tummy had to lose weight if he wanted to make the team. Willpower won the day: in two months

Puskás shed no less than eighteen kilograms (forty pounds). During his tenure with Real Madrid, the team played in five European Champion Clubs' Cup finals, of which it won three. Even though Puskás played only in three of these five games, he scored seven goals. It's hard to say whether Real Madrid would have managed to turn itself into the best club of all time without Puskás. Before his arrival, the Spanish side had two European Champion Clubs' Cup triumphs under its belt, and with the celebrated Hungarian player in its ranks it won another three. In any case, it is certain that Real Madrid's run of success in this era is bound up with Puskás's presence. In all probability, Puskás wouldn't be as well known today without the Spanish team's achievements, and by the same token, the Spaniards wouldn't have been as successful without Puskás.

After his retirement as a player at age forty, Puskás coached all over the world. His greatest success on this front was taking Panathinaikos to the European Champion Clubs' Cup final. As the only one of Hungary's defecting soccer players to be officially exonerated during the communist regime, he was able to return to his native land in 1981. In Budapest's largest stadium, the Népstadion, he dazzled fans with a remarkable diving header. Subsequently he spent most of his time in Hungary, and for a time he was head coach of the country's national team. In 2002 the Népstadion was renamed the Puskás Ferenc Stadium. After a period of ill health, Ferenc Puskás died on November 17, 2006, at the age of seventy-nine. His passing brought together Hungarians of all political persuasions in a national mourning unlike any other since the fall of communism. It marked the passing of an era, and served as a reminder that what unites this proud people is stronger than all their differences combined.

## About the Authors

**Csilla Bakody,** a graduate of Eötvös Loránd University in Budapest, was formerly a history instructor in the Hungarian Studies Division of the Balassi Institute specializing in twentieth-century Hungarian history, with a focus on the cultural politics of the interwar period.

**István Bori,** who holds degrees in geography and history from the University of Szeged, has taught since 1995 at the Balassi Institute, where he helped establish the Hungarian Studies Division. His specialties are twentieth-century Hungarian economic history and social geography.

**Nóra Csontos,** who holds a PhD in Hungarian linguistics from Eötvös Loránd University, teaches the subject as an instructor at the Balassi Institute and an assistant professor at Gáspár Károli Hungarian Reformed University. Her family's generations of experience in the hospitality sector has inspired her to also study the history of Hungarian catering and gastronomy.

**Noémi Kiss,** a writer and critic, is an assistant professor of literature at the University of Miskolc. She is the author of four books published in Hungary, including one on the poetry of Paul Celan, two collections of short stories, and a collection of travel writings.

**Jolán Mann,** a graduate of Hungarian and Croatian at Eötvös Loránd University, has been teaching Hungarian literature and cultural history since 1997 in Croatia, at the University of Zagreb. She is the literary editor of the Electronic Archives Center at the National Széchényi Library in Budapest, working on the center's Internet content service.

**Ádám Masát,** a history and political science graduate of Eötvös Loránd University, has taught since 2002 at the Balassi Institute, where since 2008 he has been a research team leader in the Hungarian Studies Division. His specialty is world history since 1945, with a focus on Germany. His doctoral dissertation concerned the Berlin Wall and the westward flight of East German refugees during the Cold War.

**Orsolya Nádor** is an associate professor of linguistics at Gáspár Károli Hungarian Reformed University and visiting professor at the University of Zagreb. She specializes in the politics surrounding the contemporary and historical development of lesser-known languages of the Carpathian Basin, Hungarian in particular; and in the history and psycholinguistic analysis of the instruction of Hungarian as a second language.

**Szabolcs Parragh** was previously an instructor of Hungarian literature and history, as well as philosophy, at various academic departments of Eötvös Loránd University, at the university's József Eötvös College, and at the Balassi Institute. Since 2008 he has earned his living as a computer programmer.

**Péter Rácz** is an award-winning poet and literary translator. His honors include the József Attila Prize (2005), the Örley Prize (1987), and a Presidential gold medal (2005). In addition to establishing two literary circles in the 1980s, he founded the Hungarian Translators House Foundation in 1995, and since 1998 has directed the Foundation's retreat in Balatonfüred, the Translators' House—an artists colony that provides space and stipends to those who translate Hungarian literature into other languages.

**Katalin Suzuki Berkes,** who earned a degree in ethnography from Eötvös Loránd University in 2002, has since been a folklore instructor at the Balassi Institute. She has published articles concerning traditional folk culture, and in particular about the lifestyle transformations over the twentieth century in regions of Hungary and environs where traditional folk culture has remained most in evidence.

**Adrienn Szentesi,** who received a degree in Hungarian language and literature from Eötvös Loránd University in 2004, taught contemporary Hungarian culture at the Balassi Institute from 2002 to 2008. Since then she has been a marketing manager at Budapest's Palace of the Arts. Her specialties include Hungarian cinema and contemporary Hungarian art.

**Gábor Vaderna,** who holds a PhD in Hungarian language and literature, is an assistant professor at Eötvös Loránd University.

## About the Balassi Institute

Based in Budapest, the Balassi Institute, named after the great Hungarian Renaissance poet Bálint Balassi (1554–1594), has a twofold mission: to expand the horizons of Hungarian culture in the wider world, and to provide opportunities for people of Hungarian descent who live outside of Hungary to nurture a genuine and fruitful relationship with the nation of their ancestry. In this spirit it organizes exhibitions, cultural events, and conferences both in Hungary and abroad. In so doing it not only devotes attention to the historic and contemporary culture of Hungarians in Hungary and those areas of the immediate vicinity that have been inhabited by Hungarians for many centuries, but also honors the distinctive characteristics of Hungarian communities throughout the world.

To realize its mission, the Balassi Institute operates nineteen cultural institutes around the globe. These offer a wide range of programs that reflect the many facets of Hungarian life while accommodating the needs and interest of the local communities.

The Balassi Institute also welcomes interested people from abroad—regardless of ancestry—to Budapest to participate in its summer university courses, language programs, and college preparatory programs. College-level instruction in Hungarian studies and literary translation is also available. Through all these activities, the Institute works toward a better understanding of Hungary in the wider world, while at the same time enriching Hungarian culture.

www.bbi.hu
Mailing address:
H-1519 Budapest
Pf. 385.
Hungary
Street address: 1016 Budapest, Somlói út 51, Hungary
Tel: 36 1 381 5100, Fax: 36 1 381 5119
Email: bbi@bbi.hu

# INDEX

(Since references are mostly brief are often repeated through a particular chapter, and the chapters are short, below we provide not page numbers but chapter numbers, from 1 to 50, as indicated in the Table of Contents. Where there are numerous incidental references, only a couple of key ones appear.)

## PEOPLE

(last name first sans comma in the case of most proper names, the Hungarian way)

## CHARACTERS FROM ORIGIN LEGENDS

## NONHUMAN BEINGS